CW00673457

"McCann and Selsky make the case that mastering turbulence is an 'ART'—a rich mix of agility, resiliency, and transformability. As resilience becomes the new sustainability, McCann and Selsky lead the way in showing why and how individuals, teams, organizations, and sectors must strike the right balance between being faster and becoming fitter, for instance, by shifting from competitive strategy and fastest growth to collaborative strategies and collective well-being. *Mastering Turbulence* is a must-read for anyone striving to navigate our hyperconnected world."

—Angela Wilkinson, director, Futures Directorate,
Smith School of Enterprise and
the Environment, Oxford University

"Turbulence in flight is the difference between falling and flying. We have come to fear turbulence in our quest to control and make our challenges seem manageable. McCann and Selsky demystify turbulence and gently guide us into a mindset to use it to help our organizations become more resilient, adaptive, and innovative."

—Richard Boyatzis, Distinguished University Professor,
Departments of Psychology, Cognitive Science and
Organizational Behavior, Case Western Reserve University;
and coauthor of the international best-sellers,
Primal Leadership and *Resonant Leadership*

"This book integrates theory and practice beautifully. The concept of adaptation is linked rigorously to a theory of turbulent environments. The result is practical advice that has the ring of experience and truth."

—Larry Hirschhorn, principal, Center for
Applied Research (CFAR)

MASTERING
TURBULENCE

Join Us at
Josseybass.com
▼

JOSSEY-BASS™
An Imprint of
WILEY

Register at **www.josseybass.com/email**
for more information on our publications,
authors, and to receive special offers.

The Jossey-Bass
Business & Management Series

MASTERING
TURBULENCE

THE ESSENTIAL CAPABILITIES OF AGILE AND RESILIENT INDIVIDUALS, TEAMS, AND ORGANIZATIONS

JOSEPH McCANN AND JOHN W. SELSKY

Foreword by Jay Jamrog

JOSSEY-BASS
A Wiley Imprint
www.josseybass.com

Copyright © 2012 by John Wiley & Sons, Inc. All rights reserved.

Published by Jossey-Bass
A Wiley Imprint
One Montgomery Street, Suite 1200, San Francisco, CA 94104-4594—www.josseybass.com

No part of this publication may be reproduced, stored in a retrieval system, or transmitted in any form or by any means, electronic, mechanical, photocopying, recording, scanning, or otherwise, except as permitted under Section 107 or 108 of the 1976 United States Copyright Act, without either the prior written permission of the publisher, or authorization through payment of the appropriate per-copy fee to the Copyright Clearance Center, Inc., 222 Rosewood Drive, Danvers, MA 01923, 978-750-8400, fax 978-646-8600, or on the Web at www.copyright.com. Requests to the publisher for permission should be addressed to the Permissions Department, John Wiley & Sons, Inc., 111 River Street, Hoboken, NJ 07030, 201-748-6011, fax 201-748-6008, or online at www.wiley.com/go/permissions.

Limit of Liability/Disclaimer of Warranty: While the publisher and author have used their best efforts in preparing this book, they make no representations or warranties with respect to the accuracy or completeness of the contents of this book and specifically disclaim any implied warranties of merchantability or fitness for a particular purpose. No warranty may be created or extended by sales representatives or written sales materials. The advice and strategies contained herein may not be suitable for your situation. You should consult with a professional where appropriate. Neither the publisher nor author shall be liable for any loss of profit or any other commercial damages, including but not limited to special, incidental, consequential, or other damages. Readers should be aware that Internet Web sites offered as citations and/or sources for further information may have changed or disappeared between the time this was written and when it is read.

Jossey-Bass books and products are available through most bookstores. To contact Jossey-Bass directly call our Customer Care Department within the U.S. at 800-956-7739, outside the U.S. at 317-572-3986, or fax 317-572-4002.

Wiley publishes in a variety of print and electronic formats and by print-on-demand. Some material included with standard print versions of this book may not be included in e-books or in print-on-demand. If this book refers to media such as a CD or DVD that is not included in the version you purchased, you may download this material at http://booksupport.wiley.com. For more information about Wiley products, visit www.wiley.com.

Library of Congress Cataloging-in-Publication Data
McCann, Joseph E.
   Mastering turbulence: the essential capabilities of agile and resilient individuals, teams, and organizations / Joseph McCann and John W. Selsky; foreword by Jay Jamrog. —First edition.
      pages cm. —(The Jossey-Bass business & management series)
   Includes bibliographical references and index.
   ISBN 978-1-118-16483-9 (hardcover); ISBN 978-1-118-22623-0 (ebk); ISBN 978-1-118-23955-1 (ebk); ISBN 978-1-118-26417-1 (ebk)
   1. Organizational change—Management.   I. Selsky, John W. II. Title.
   HD58.8.M3327 2012
   658.4'06—dc23

                  2012016813

Printed in the United States of America
FIRST EDITION
HB Printing 10 9 8 7 6 5 4 3 2 1

CONTENTS

LIST OF FIGURES, TABLES, AND EXHIBITS

Figures

Tables

Exhibits

FOREWORD

J oe and John take on a formidable and critical challenge with this book. I have encouraged and followed their research over the past years with great interest. I can confidently say that *Mastering Turbulence* is a major contribution in furthering our efforts at managing environmental turbulence. With the increasing number and scale of surprises and shocks, disruptive change is now intertwined with rapid change. This combination is creating such turbulent conditions that sustainable high performance is becoming extremely difficult to achieve.

As they stress, there is little question that the performance of individuals, teams, organizations, and their ecosystems is being severely compromised. Whether disengaged employees, compromised leadership teams, slow responses to organizational opportunities and threats, or fragile supply chains and industries, the effects of increasing turbulence can be devastating.

Yet, as Joe and John clearly establish, not everyone is in the same boat. Many prosper during turbulence and it is their agility and resiliency that make a difference. There are several specific capabilities which they explore in very unique, detailed ways that promote agility and resiliency. However, organizations must accept two key prerequisites: agility and resiliency have to be developed together—what Joe and John call High AR—and at four levels—

individual, team, organization, and ecosystem. These prerequisites differentiate their work from anything else in the change management literature that I know.

Mastering Turbulence makes its greatest contribution, however, when it explores five capabilities that High AR organizations possess: they are Being Purposeful, Being Aware, Being Action-Oriented, Being Resourceful, and Being Networked. Each of these capabilities has its own chapter, and each chapter offers unique, frame-breaking concepts and models that require thoughtful consideration. Helpful organization stories and examples are provided throughout the book to illustrate those concepts and practices.

Finally, Joe and John recognize the formidable development challenge they create for leadership teams. They define the key roles and responsibilities of the major actors in their last chapter and provide a survey instrument for organization use in an Appendix. My predecessor organization to i4cp, HRI, applied many of those items in an earlier research study, but the survey provided in their Appendix takes research into agility and resiliency into entirely new domains with its focus on the five capabilities. In the collaborative spirit for which they are known, Joe and John invite readers to apply and share survey results in the effort to develop reliable tools for assessing and improving agility and resiliency.

Improving our capabilities for mastering turbulence must be one of the highest priorities for organizations today. The quality of life and continued performance of the individuals and teams within them, and an organization's capacity for collaborative action depend on accepting this priority. *Mastering Turbulence* provides an important path forward.

Jay Jamrog
Senior Vice President, Research
i4cp
St. Petersburg and Seattle

PREFACE

We are on a twenty-five-year quest to understand the strategies needed for managing increasingly rapid, disruptive change. This quest is driven by the deep concern that leaders are doing a fantastic though unintentional job of building highly fragile organizations that are overexposed to turbulent change; their performance compromised, many are destined to fail. The individuals and teams within them, charged with sustaining their high performance, are just as compromised and fragile. And as organizations become weakened, they drop out of collaborative efforts to deal with shared issues, thus compromising the larger ecosystems in which they must operate.

Can you actually "master" turbulence, as our title suggests? Before you launch into a book that takes you to as many places as this one is about to do, that is a fair question to ask. First, you cannot ever master turbulence once and for all. By definition, change constantly mutates and is so pervasive that it intrudes into all aspects of organizational life. But you can work at it with skill and persistence, which is why we use the term "mastering" turbulence; it is a process, not an outcome. Managers of all kinds and at all levels of organizations, both private sector and public sector, have to make forceful attempts at improving their management of turbulence. The consequences, as this book illustrates, are otherwise simply too severe.

Second, there is consensus that it is getting tougher to sustain high levels of performance, either personal or organizational, when the pace and disruptiveness of change is so relentless. Yet, as we will point out, the fact is that some managers and executives and some organizations are doing so very well. These "others" have apparently developed higher-order capabilities that are making a clear difference in their success.

Finally, greater investments in new technologies and skills certainly help, and mastering turbulence is also very much about working smarter, not just harder. New mental models, conceptual perspectives, and ways of managing can give managers the leverage they need to build a real and sustainable adaptive capacity. This book is largely about those models, perspectives, and practices. We define the topography and terrain for the work needed and largely avoid specific tools and techniques. In this sense, our book is designed for thoughtful readers who can best benefit from having the big picture and key intervention targets identified, but either already have the requisite tools and techniques at hand or know how and where to acquire them.

This is our starting point. It will be challenging for you to sweep across the necessary range of topics covered, which is precisely why it is so difficult to master turbulence. But this is why we wrote this book—to bring many of the essential elements together in one place. The answers we provide are not simple, and you may find them challenging, but the consequences of not making an attempt to learn them are even greater.

This book is about what we have learned regarding some of the capabilities that organizations, along with their individuals and teams, need for not just managing but also mastering environmental turbulence and sustaining high performance. When these capabilities are highly developed, we know that organizations can even use turbulence to build their competitive advantage. We have found some essential capabilities to be well known and in use, whereas others are not and require much faster development. All of them must be applied more thoughtfully and strategically than ever before. This book helps organizations do just that.

The reason is that the terrain today for many businesses—as well as governments and nonprofit organizations—is chaotic, multilayered, and richly textured. It is, in short, turbulent. Sometimes the turbulence comes in short bursts—the Australian dollar shoots up by 25 percent in six months, or global supply chains are compromised by a tsunami in Japan. Sometimes the turbulence is chronic—a financial crisis drags on, morphs in unexpected ways, and links with additional unstable situations in ways that seemed implausible a short while ago. How in the world did problems in the U.S. subprime mortgage market in 2007 produce a dire threat to the very existence of the European Union in 2011? Turbulence in the external environment disrupts single organizations, rocks industries, and unsettles entire policy sectors alike. This is why it is important to understand turbulence and deal with it swiftly. For a business, its competitive performance in its industry is at risk; for a governmental or nonprofit entity, at risk is its legitimacy vis-à-vis its constituencies and stakeholders.

This is no time for muddling through. Nor is it time to hunker down until the hurricane blows past. Personally, we were first amused then disturbed by the number of executives and CNBC pundits explaining away the trillions of dollars sidelined by corporations who believed conditions were "too uncertain" for investing in the economy in 2011. As if this uncertainty is going to diminish! It isn't—welcome, indeed, to the "new normal."

This is not *terra incognita* for authors writing books for practicing managers. There are many such books and they follow a formula. First, titillate the reader with the importance of the problem (outsourcing! loss of competitiveness! climate change! technology run amok! competition run amok! dispirited employees run amok!). Next, establish credibility that *you* have the key insight into the problem. Then, proffer a framework that turns your insight into a no-nonsense or elegant solution set, and make recommendations that only the astute manager will be able to understand and implement. Finally, wrap it up with a glimpse of an even scarier future if your solution is not adopted. This is the well-worn path to modest business book success.

We want to challenge this formula in our book because the terrain is becoming so complex and dynamic that we are legitimately concerned about how well turbulence will be managed. For many organizations, the environment is *not* stable and neither is their competitive situation. They are turbulent in the special sense we describe in Chapter One. The magnitude of this issue—forces of profound disruption and chaos buffeting organizations, industries, and policy sectors of all shapes and sizes—calls for a big, expansive response.

Hence our sources are quite diverse and eclectic—rock songs, blogs, and newspapers in addition to executive interviews, and, perhaps unfortunately, many academic citations. The citations are here for a reason. The topics covered range from the latest advances in brain chemistry and neuroscience to global supply chains and innovation clusters; we offer these resources for readers to pursue their interests beyond what we can do here.

The citations are also consistent with our own academic training. The mentors and professors we studied with—Eric Trist, Russell Ackoff, and others at Wharton and elsewhere—were magnificent thinkers, with their feet planted firmly on the ground of field-based practice with some of the world's most successful companies. Eric, especially, was first and foremost an action researcher, working with a wide range of characters and organizations, whether in English coal mines or devastated industrial communities in upstate New York. We think their basic message was right; systems thinking is a powerful tool for making sense of what philosopher William James called "a great big buzzing confusion."

As a result of our background and training, the conceptual framework we offer is big and encompassing. We believe that highly agile and resilient systems are Purposeful, Aware, Action-Oriented, Resourceful, and intelligently Networked. These five capabilities must be worked in a strategic, systematic way at four levels—individual, team, organization, and ecosystem. This creates a rich 4 × 5 matrix that managers and executives can use to develop agility and resiliency, and thereby their high performance, in the turbulent environments they face. We present this framework through the first three chapters and then, over the five chapters that follow, illustrate how the five capabilities play critical roles in achieving agility and resiliency. Finally, we bring the elements together in the last chapter, addressing the basic question of managerial and executive roles and responsibilities for developing agility and resiliency through the capabilities.

We think this multilevel approach to the requirements for high performance is a distinctive feature of our book. Taking a purely organizational level focus on managing turbulence is simply unrealistic. First, it ignores the people inside the organization who are struggling mightily with turbulence in their own personal lives and in the workgroups in which they participate. Second, it ignores that great amorphous area on the other side of an increasingly permeable organizational boundary, what we call the ecosystem. This is where managers can work, in concert with others, to shape the external context. For despite calls for organizations to foster cooperative strategies and partnerships, we think the ecosystem level remains seriously underdeveloped.

We believe this is a dangerous gap when turbulent environments are prevalent, because the contextual disruptions in such environments impinge upon an organization only *through* its interdependencies with others in its ecosystem. Ecosystems are the external contexts in which organizations operate, such as the industry, supply chain, policy sectors (for example, health care and education), or the organization's home community and region. Adding the ecosystem level to our framework was especially challenging, but we felt it was crucial. Ultimately, doing so was rewarding because it forced us to sharpen our thinking about how organizations work with others across organizational boundaries, and how they can push those boundaries outward by collaborating with others to create more defensible, less turbulent space. When members of an ecosystem act in concert on shared issues, they build agility and resiliency at the level of their ecosystem.

We could have written an entire book just about agility, or just about resiliency, but either would have been seriously lacking. Our research with several hundred organizations confirms that the two concepts are strongly correlated and integral dimensions of adaptive capacity. We are, after all, writing this book late in 2011, ten years after the shocking events of September 11, 2001. Perhaps this one-decade anniversary is an apt commentary on the core theme of the book. It is now the received wisdom, at least in the United States, that 9/11 changed everything. It does seem to have gradually changed the way that managers view their external environments. The events of ten years ago occurred at the tail end of the Clinton-era boom and the dot-com bust that followed it. The loud message through this period was that organizations needed to be as agile, flexible, and speedy as possible to remain viable in hypercompetitive markets.

September 11 put the brakes on this headlong charge. In the new security environment, "hardening," "defending," and "withstanding" have become more frequent dictums. One of our early inspirations for this work was a paper devoted to exploring and explaining the recovery of Sandler O'Neill LLC, a securities trading company housed in the World Trade Center, after its staff and resources were decimated in the 9/11 attack. The paper focused

on the resiliency of key staff at the firm. It was written by colleagues of ours—Steve Freeman, Larry Hirschhorn, and Marc
Maltz (2004), and we are indebted to them for inspiring our thinking about the need to consider agility and resiliency together. We
refer to this case in several chapters.

Agility and resiliency are likely not the only capabilities that
require hard thinking and development into useful tools that can
help managers to master their own destinies. There are others,
we're sure, but these are immensely powerful concepts and merit
your attention here.

Joseph McCann and John W. Selsky
Indian Rocks Beach and Lakeland, Florida

To the memory of Eric L. Trist (1909–1993)—mentor, colleague, life-long inspiration.

ACKNOWLEDGMENTS

We wish to acknowledge the following people who helped us in this project in various ways. They are listed in alphabetical order:

Clint Childress
Alexis Fink
Steve Hanks
John Hogan
David Graham Hyatt
Jay Jamrog
Jim Lee
Aaron Maniam
Marti McCann
Josiah Pritchard
Bruce Rennie
Mark Vickers
Alan Warnick
Peter West
Jeana Wirtenberg
USF Polytechnic students in John's Fall 2011 Organization
    Assessment class and his colleagues in the Innovation
    Management Division

MASTERING
TURBULENCE

chapter
ONE

Turbulence Crossing the Channel

Rapid change has been a feature of our world for decades, driven by technological innovation across nearly every culture and feature of a globalizing economy. If we revisit the landmark books written over thirty and forty years ago by Alvin and Heidi Toffler, *Future Shock* in 1970 and *The Third Wave* in 1980, we see just how insightful they were as turbulence began cranking up during the transformation from an industrial to information technology age. Early signs were already heralded in the 1960s with the term "turbulent environment" launched by Fred Emery and Eric Trist in 1965 (see Exhibit 1.1). However, it was not just the pace of change that they saw early on, but the disruptiveness of the current change we are experiencing. Rapid, disruptive change is now creating a level of unprecedented turbulence that is challenging organizations more than ever before.

As Chapter Two explains, we used to view a period of more rapid or extensive change simply as a deviation from normal

Exhibit 1.1. Turbulence over the Channel

The word "turbulence" has become one of the most common words used to describe rapid and disruptive change, but do you ever wonder how it came to this use? One of the earliest and most heavily cited sources was in Fred Emery and Eric Trist's article in *Human Relations,* "The Causal Texture of Organizational Environments" (1965), which described how four different types of environments evolved. They rarely told the story to their students or visitors, but it seems that Eric and Fred were flying from Europe to London on a particularly rough flight. On Eric's tabletop was a newspaper dealing with all the tragedies of those mid-sixties days. A cup of tea was set on the paper and promptly spilled as the plane bounced about. Now whether the cup had tea in it or something more typical for that duo is subject to debate among those who knew them. Nonetheless, they had been looking for a word to describe the fourth and most troubling type of environmental condition they had theorized when it became obvious that they had just experienced it. The concept of environmental turbulence to describe a human-experienced condition was introduced into the management literature on a bumpy flight across the English Channel.

operating conditions, predictable as a choreographed annual new car rollout from Detroit or a plant retooling. Internal operations were also nicely buffered by inventories and slack resources such as extra staff or money tucked away in a business unit's operating budget. Once the change ripple passed, the organization could return to normal operations. True, there were competitive countermoves and business cycles, but these were normal noise and readily managed.

This type of predict-and-prepare change management unfortunately could not last. The exponential pace of technological change in nearly every field, particularly information and communications technologies, occurred just as new competitors, new industries, even entire new trading blocs of nations with different cultural world views and expectations, formed a global economy.

The rest, as the saying goes, is history, and we are all now faced not only by fast change, but change in the form of severe shocks and surprises—events that arrive with unanticipated frequency and from entirely unexpected sources—that not only disrupt plans and strategies but threaten the very viability of organizations and institutions. If there is a return to "normal," it is hopefully not what PIMCO's Bill Gross in the summer of 2009 termed the "New Normal"—a period of prolonged high unemployment, blocked credit, and lower asset returns and expectations where the economic shocks of the Great Recession are felt for a generation (R. Cohen, 2010). Such a prospect is unsettling because it means having to face other potential new shocks from an already weakened position. There is the prospect of a long-term debilitating cycle that is missing the normal slower paced, less disruptive time periods needed for recovery. Turbulence has become our new normal.

Why is disruptive change becoming a growing part of our experience? It seems to be very much like the shifting tectonic plate conditions that generate earthquakes. Disruptiveness is caused by uneven rates of change among the interdependent elements and relationships at play in a situation. Such interdependencies and relationships pose contingencies, rich with risks and advantages that have to be recognized and actively managed. Left unrecognized and undermanaged, these interdependencies create frictions and tensions that are periodically unleashed in the form of surprises and shocks, just like earthquakes. However, earthquakes for people and organizations show up as collapsing twin towers, a financial system near collapse and lingering Great Recession, or successive ecological disasters, whether a BP Gulf of Mexico oil rig or leaking Fukushima nuclear reactors.

Events like these now feel like they are coming more closely packed than ever before. The abrasion of technology-based Western democratic cultures against traditional cultures is intense and recognized as a source of militant Islamic resentment toward the West. Any jet-lagged Western soul sitting in a hotel room in Dubai watching late-night television is dismayed by the portrayal of Western society. Or consider the tensions being built and yet to be released when there are no toilets but thousands of cell phones in some of India's worst slums. And who could have anticipated Facebook- and Twitter-facilitated government upheavals in Egypt and elsewhere in the Middle East? The Tofflers and any number of other futurists could forecast that new fault lines would be created and tensions built in such situations. How those tensions would be released was impossible to say.

Our concern is that the change management challenge for leaders has fundamentally transformed to the point that we are trying to manage new conditions and situations with outmoded institutional practices and structures designed for a much less complex and dynamic time. A dangerously flawed lapse in institutional leadership is manifest in the inability or unwillingness to proactively and creatively manage situations where tensions are clearly building; such tensions are only released in sudden and unpredictable ways. In his book *Beyond the Crash: Overcoming the First Crisis of Globalization* (2010), former British prime minister Sir Gordon Brown calls this mismatch of conditions and adaptive capacity "a failure of collective action," that is, the failure of institutional structures to keep pace with turbulence. We are simply not adapting as quickly, proactively, or effectively as the times demand.

Indeed, even the word *adaptation* is now undergoing an interesting shift in meaning. There is a growing sense, for example, that the world's political institutions cannot create the working consensus necessary to prevent or mitigate global climate change. This is reflected in IPCC reports since the late 1990s. Instead, more and more companies believe that they must learn to adapt to the unavoidable *consequences* of climate change, rather than prevent it. Starbucks, for example, is creating incentives for its coffee growers to halt soil erosion and to minimize total water use throughout its supply chain. As Jim Hanna, Starbucks's director of environmental impact, notes, "Adaptation is becoming part of our strategy" (Efstathiou & Chipman, 2010, p. 25). In this context, such strategy is reactive, not proactive, in that it is attempting to manage the *consequences,* not *causes,* of global climate change. Using our vocabulary, Starbucks has clearly increased its attention to the resiliency of its supply chain.

The litany of events brought about by disruptive change is growing and has several sources. They include man-made events such as 9/11; the BP oil spill in the Gulf of Mexico in 2010; drawn-out, resource-bleeding wars in Iraq and Afghanistan; and, as we write this in early 2012, a protracted global financial crisis that is permanently tilting the global economic balance of power. There are also natural events. In 2010 alone the massive earthquake in Haiti was followed too quickly by devastating floods across Pakistan that overwhelmed the capacities of NGOs, international institutions, and friendly governments to meet all of the financial and humanitarian needs that arose.

Attention spans, resources, and efforts are spread out and stretched, further limiting the full capacity to act as fresh disruptions occur. The Fukushima nuclear disaster's ultimate impact remains unknown as we write this book. However, some consequences were already being felt, as Reuter's James Topham wrote on April 25, 2011, that Toyota Motor Company would fall to the number three from the number one position in global car production as a result of supply disruptions from the disaster (Topham, 2011).

Our early concerns about turbulent change led to the design of a global survey about agility and resiliency that was cosponsored by the Human Resource Institute (now Institute for Corporate Productivity or i4cp) and American Management Association/Human Resources Institute (AMA/HRI) (2006). Eighty percent of the more than eight hundred organizations responding to the survey reported an increasing pace of change that, while still manageable, was becoming more challenging. Significantly, 70 percent of respondents also reported increases in the number of surprises and severe shocks that necessitated changes in their business strategies. Figure 1.1 summarizes those findings and breaks them out by performance levels, measured as profitability and competitiveness. The difference between perceptions among higher and lower performers is striking and helped direct our subsequent work, as we explain in a moment.

Figure 1.1. Perceived Pace and Predictability of Change

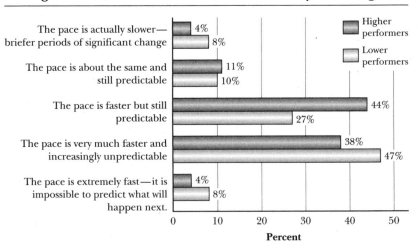

Source: American Management Association/Human Resources Institute, 2006.

The intense interaction between accelerating change and increasing surprises and shocks creates dynamics that are relatively new on the human stage. Many organizations do not know how to handle this degree of turbulence well. As Martin Ford notes in his 2009 book *The Lights in the Tunnel: Automation, Technology & the Economy of the Future,* "As we will see, technology is not just advancing gradually, it is accelerating. As a result, the impact may come long before we expect it—and long before we are ready" (Ford, 2009, p. 6). So it is not surprising that mistakes will be made by leaders in organizations when they realize, too late, that outbreaks of turbulence are absorbing more and more resources to manage them and setbacks and failures are increasing.

We are unfortunately seeing leaders making choices and taking actions for managing turbulence that are not only misplaced and ineffective, but even threatening to their long-term survival. One characteristic of increasing turbulence is that it is coming from "out there," outside the realm of our personal and organizational control and influence—that is, the sources or manifestations of turbulence are contextual or exogenous. For leaders used to controlling events, it is decidedly disorienting to feel control slipping away.

With the past popularity of such books as Richard D'Aveni's *Hypercompetition: Managing the Dynamics of Strategic Maneuvering* (1994) and Clayton Christensen's *Innovator's Dilemma: When New Technologies Cause Great Firms to Fail* (1997), it is clear that organizations want to act aggressively and proactively in shaping their competitive markets. However, a good portion of the turbulence these same organizations now experience is being *self-induced* by their own unilateral competitive acts that interact with others' similar unilateral actions. We end up contributing to conditions that we never expected to have to manage.

Note another very important feature of turbulence: events intersect and reinforce each other, creating political, social, and economic eddies and whirlpools that magnify their complexity and seeming intractability. Few issues or challenges presented by turbulence are simple. Issues are tangled in a knot of interdependencies that makes complexity one of the most defining characteristics of turbulent environments. As former U.S. senator Bob Graham, an appointed member of the committee investigating the 2010 BP Gulf disaster, noted in a hearing reported on National Public Radio, "Complex systems fail in complex ways." Eric Bonabeau, an expert on complexity theory, had prophetically noted three years earlier, "In fact, catastrophic events are almost guaranteed to occur in many complex systems, much like big earthquakes are bound to happen. Indeed, the statistics of events in manmade systems is starting to closely resemble that of destructive natural phenomena" (Bonabeau, 2007).

There is a growing sense that organizations are losing control of their operating environments—the ecosystems in which their immediate suppliers, customers, communities, and other stakeholders interact. These operating domains are being subjected to turbulence induced in their larger contextual environments, which are now taking on dynamics all their own. When morning rioting in Athens over the Greek government's austerity moves limits access to credit that afternoon for small businesses in Omaha, it is turbulence in the contextual environment affecting the entire global financial sector—and more.

This tight connection between contextual and operating environments is certainly not new. The SARS outbreak in China over a decade ago halted computer plants in California for several days, even weeks, as global supply chains shut down. The Japan earthquake and Fukushima disaster did the same, just for a much longer time period.

The fact is that we are not just connected; we are "hyperconnected" (Retter, 2001) with too many interdependencies—many unrecognized, many unwanted—all demanding active attention if we are to manage the risks associated with them and remain successful. When Starbucks or ArcelorMittal, the world's largest coffee retailer and steel producer, respectively, built tight global supply chains and vertically integrated production systems, they may have reduced their exposure to market price volatility for coffee and iron ore, but those systems required billions of dollars of investment and demand ongoing, active management. Reducing the risks and impact associated with turbulence is costly.

Welcome to Hyperturbulence

What is unique about this predicament, however, is how it is playing out at multiple levels, all of which are integrally linked and dependent on each other. We talk about organizational agility and resiliency, but we marvel at the fact that it is the individuals and teams of individuals functioning within them that really must bear the impact of turbulence. At an individual level, people feel the effects when the number and variety of events they have to deal with become so mind-numbing that they develop high levels of stress and anxiety. Health suffers, psychological burnout becomes the norm, and dissociative behaviors (the "flight" side of the "fight-or-flight" response) prevail. As Richard Eckersley noted in *The Futurist*: "The images we hold of the world affect how we think, feel, and act, and they are increasingly shaped by global and distant threat and disaster. . . . While these hazards are, for the most part, not new, previous fears were never so sustained and varied, nor so powerfully reinforced by the frequency, immediacy, and vividness of today's media images. . . . The boundaries between the personal and the global are breaking down" (Eckersley, 2008, p. 35).

This new intimate linkage between the personal and the global plays out at work, at home, and in communities. In the workplace the effects of turbulence are felt at the team level of work groups when economic distress forces cutbacks, destroying skilled technical work teams in Detroit auto factories, and threatening a whole generation of the U.S. workforce with underemployment.

For individuals, these new forces can also mean forsaking the idea of work-life "balance" and accepting work-life "integration" or even "no life" as the norm. Our communications technologies are now inseparably parts of our personal life and intrude relentlessly. Like all features of change, this is good and bad at the same time. Indeed, as Thomas Friedman points out in *The World Is Flat: A Brief History of the Twenty-first Century* (2005), it is a defining characteristic of turbulence that individuals are now active players at a global level. Whether it is a solo terrorist in London or a Bangladeshi farmer linked to global commodity markets via a cheap cell phone, power is being decentralized into the hands of individuals. We are adjusting to a global workday where someone, somewhere, is always working ahead of us or after us while we sleep. It is an uneasy sleep.

We also see the effects of undermanaged turbulence at the organization level when profits suffer, innovation seizes up, companies fail, and valuable networks of suppliers collapse. And we see the impacts at the broadest levels, such as in the global financial system, when the economic vitality of a small nation like Greece can be questioned and a trillion dollars of global market equity is lost in a matter of days. The U.S. Army War College coined the acronym VUCA to refer to a world that was Volatile, Uncertain, Complex, and Ambiguous; that pretty well sums up the conditions facing us (Horney, Pasmore, & O'Shea, 2010).

Our own concern is that we are edging closer to a condition we tagged in 1984 as "hyperturbulence"—too many and too frequent surprises and shocks that they simply overwhelm the adaptive capacity of individuals, teams, and organizations to manage. As Chapter Two discusses, environmental change evolved from manageable episodic change where temporary changes punctuated normal operating conditions, to continuous rapid change that required more significant and frequent

Figure 1.2. Severity of Impact from Three Kinds of Change

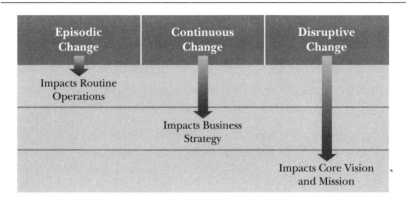

shifts in business strategies, to disruptive change that is potentially so challenging that it threatens the very identity and viability of the organization and those that support it (Selsky & McCann, 2008). Figure 1.2 illustrates this idea of change penetrating deeper into the core of the organization as it has evolved (Bouchikhi & Kimberly, 2003).

As organizations encounter increasingly rapid and disruptive change, simply responding with shifts in operations and business strategies is not enough. Much more is demanded, yet the available repertoire of adaptive strategies is not up to the task. We are finding too many examples of anemic strategies being deployed today. We should never approach the point where we have so few response choices. Our recommendations are designed to significantly expand that set of effective responses.

Change as Opportunity

There is a fascinating paradox to all this that gave us the insight we needed to create a positive, motivating story to tell. While many are reeling from turbulent change, there are many others who view these dynamic operating conditions opportunistically and as sources of competitive advantage. What sped us along our current path of inquiry was the global survey we conducted and subsequent research that provided clear evidence that higher-performing organizations, in terms of profitability and competitiveness, perceive their environments as both more manageable and providing more opportunities to shake things up to their advantage (McCann, Selsky, & Lee, 2009). The converse was also true—lower-performing organizations experienced their environments as more challenging and were more reactive than proactive toward change. This was illustrated in Figure 1.1 by the differences between higher- and lower-performing organizations. Our conclusion? Not everybody is in the same boat. It is clear that turbulence is not experienced evenly.

We were intrigued by what makes rapid and disruptive change so hazardous for some and such an opportunity for others. What we have learned is that the actual effects of such change depend on the amount and nature of the adaptive capacity available to manage it. Simple enough, but adaptive capacity is a multifaceted concept with many attributes and elements. It's one of those concepts that everyone may use, but is very complex to operationalize.

So what are the aspects or features of adaptive capacity that must be specifically targeted? Agility and resiliency are two of the most critical elements or attributes we have found for sustaining, even building, superior performance in the midst of increasing turbulence. Chapter Two provides a context for understanding the role of agility and resiliency as elements of adaptive capacity, and both concepts are thoroughly developed in Chapter Three.

These concepts have been getting exceptional attention in the management literature and media for some time now, for obvious reasons. Much of this literature is thoughtful; however, much of it is, honestly, muddled. Based on our own research and work with organizations, we believe that we now understand some of the most important new features of agility and resiliency.

We found that agility and resiliency are conceptually and statistically unique concepts or constructs, but they are highly correlated with each other. That is, both are distinct and essential elements of adaptive capacity, and it is impossible, even dangerous, to consider developing one without the other. They must be considered as two sides of the same coin and we approach them as an integrated concept—"AR"—from this point forward. Chapter Three provides the rationale and logic for developing "High AR" at four deeply interconnected levels—individual, team, organization, and the organization's larger business ecosystem.

Chapter Three also describes the characteristics of High AR individuals, teams, organizations, and ecosystems in terms of five critical capabilities. These individuals, teams, organizations, and their ecosystems are: Being Purposeful, Being Aware, Being Action-Oriented, Being Resourceful, and Being Networked. These five capabilities are manifested in many similar and different forms across all four of these levels. Figure 1.3 illustrates the idea that these five capabilities are the basis for AR. They have to be considered together as a bundle of capabilities that are most powerful when individually developed to their full potential and then tightly integrated with each other. Overall, AR is greatest when this occurs; both agility and resiliency are enhanced. On the other hand, AR is compromised when one or more are not developed and integrated well with the others.

This is what our book is about—building and sustaining high performance in turbulent environments by developing these five critical capabilities across all four levels. It is simply not effective or realistic to think that you can sustain organization performance by focusing on one or two of these capabilities; it is equally ineffective and unrealistic to think that operating at just one or two levels will work either. A more strategic perspective and approach is necessary.

Figure 1.3. The Five Essential Capabilities for High AR

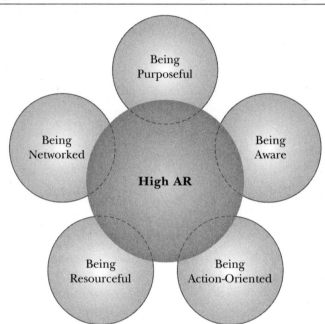

An organizing model is provided in Chapter Three to help guide thinking and action for developing High AR. As we noted in the Preface, ours is not a simple model, but it does capture how capabilities and levels work with each other. Chapters Four through Eight describe each of these capabilities in detail and provide specific strategies and intervention points for building them. Chapter Four makes the case that Being Purposeful promotes High AR, because it is founded on a clear and firmly held core identity, supported by physical, psychological, and social wellness. We believe that being and acting purposeful, particularly at the individual level and team level, is the foundational capability. For this reason, Chapter Four is also one of the longest chapters in this book.

Chapter Five focuses on Being Aware to promote High AR in terms of the essential competencies, knowledge, and skills that support organizational learning and effective knowledge management. In turn, it is organizational learning and knowledge management that underlie critical sensemaking practices and processes that support timely and appropriate action.

Chapter Six builds the argument that High AR also requires Being Action-Oriented—a capability typically associated with agility and resiliency in the literature. Without question, being capable of swift, flexible, and sustained action to seize opportunities and minimize or avoid the negative impact of events is an important part of this capability. However, that is too simplistic. Guiding such action must be an adaptive design mindset that focuses much, much more on what we call a "roll-up and rollout" model that matches the characteristics and experiences of individuals' knowledge, skills, and core competencies with the organization's strategies. Other skills are also called for in that chapter, including strategic boundary management, which essentially calls for triaging stakeholder relationships to consciously manage their value and risks.

Chapter Seven similarly focuses on a capability often associated with agility and resiliency—Being Resourceful. Being Resourceful means thinking creatively and acting entrepreneurially at all levels, but in different ways using different scripts, as we call them, that meet the conditions facing the organization. We offer four such scripts, although others certainly exist. Our objective is to drive home the idea that the environmental conditions presented an organization require differentiated responses if the outcome is to be optimized as an opportunity, or minimized or avoided entirely, if a threat.

Chapter Eight recognizes that High AR is very much a function of the quality of the networks of relationships that exist at all four levels in our model. Being Networked for High AR entails an awareness that action always occurs through others. Being able to call on others in a valuable, carefully managed network for support in time of need can make the difference in how well opportunity is realized or damage minimized. That support may take many forms—in knowledge and skills, finances, or effort. Indeed, we argue that the domain for action has shifted to collaborative networks of actors as ways of creating innovative solutions, aligning unilateral actions, and establishing more defensible shared space.

Chapter Nine brings all the pieces together with specific recommendations for sustaining a strategic AR perspective, creating significant organization change expertise, and making sure that all of that management effort is used well. The roles and responsibilities of the key actors involved in building High AR are also described.

This formidable development challenge requires thoughtfully aligning and constantly balancing these capabilities across all four levels. We try to provide numerous stories and examples as illustrations in all of these chapters about the challenges, strategies, and skills involved.

chapter
TWO

The Origins and Consequences of Turbulence

Chapter One provided you a rationale for why building adaptive capacity is essential for sustaining high performance as turbulence increases. We noted that our field research on several hundred organizations revealed how higher levels of agility and resiliency—both critical dimensions of adaptive capacity—are associated with higher organization competitiveness and profitability. Being able to take advantage of opportunities quickly and avoid damaging collisions with events can translate directly into improved profitability and competitiveness, particularly when others are not able to do so as quickly and effectively.

We stated that strategically building the five capabilities associated with agility and resiliency at four levels—individual, team, organization, and ecosystem—helps develop essential adaptive capacity. Adaptive capacity is to organizations what the immune system is to humans. The credibility of this case rests on a basic assumption that rapid and disruptive change is increasing to a point where many organizations' future strategies and tactics for managing change are not working as effectively as in the past. New conditions demand novel perspectives and tools. An energetic search is now on for concepts and models capable of explaining what is happening in organizational environments and helping organizations continue achieving superior performance.

The tremendous investment in legacy concepts, models, and management mindsets, so broadly manifested in prevailing organization designs and processes, complicates this search. With their entrenched regulatory systems, governance hierarchies, and operating routines, organizations have not been designed for transformative change unless severely threatened. Many even aspire to the institutional legitimacy of a General Motors or AIG— the infamous "too big to fail" status.

How would you design an organization for creative, adaptive change? Over the past forty years there has been a rapid evolution in management thinking which provides a powerful vantage point for exploring this question. This chapter describes how past management thinking, particularly systems theory, has shaped organizations' design choices up to this point. It is also a launching point for helping you understand why agility and resiliency have now become such critical design elements. We will use the basic vocabulary of core concepts shown in Table 2.1 because the literature has been very ambiguous.

Evolution of Organizations as Systems

The adoption of general systems theory (GST) concepts from biology and physics into management studies has been one of the most important events in at least fifty years. Systems thinking,

Table 2.1. Key Definitions

Environmental Turbulence	The pace and disruptiveness of change within an operational, competitive, or larger contextual environment.
Pace of Change	Variations in the frequency, number, and kinds of conditions being experienced.
Disruptive Change	Severe surprises and unanticipated shocks that destabilize performance, even threaten ongoing viability.
Adaptive Capacity	The amount and variety of resources and skills possessed and available for maintaining viability and growth relative to the requirements posed by the environment.
Agility	The capacity for moving quickly, flexibly, and decisively in anticipating, initiating, and taking advantage of opportunities and avoiding any negative consequences of change.
Resiliency	The capacity for resisting, absorbing, and responding, even reinventing if required, in response to fast and/or disruptive change that cannot be avoided.

Source: McCann, Selsky, & Lee, 2009.

the corollary mindset for systems theory, assumes that a situation is best understood by looking at it in its larger context, and the concept has spread widely in rhetoric, if not in practice.

Actually, we personally find systems thinking in pretty short supply, but there are reasons why that is the case. Later chapters talk about the threat-rigidity response, but the idea is essentially that organisms—human or organizational—tend to hunker down when threatened and sustained turbulence intuitively evokes that reaction. We will argue that a better response to sustained turbulence is precisely counterintuitive—lift your head high, look around, and engage with others in managing it. For that to be effective requires building the kinds of capabilities we are writing about.

Russell L. Ackoff's final book, *Systems Thinking for Curious Managers* (2010), provides a good sampling of ideas associated with systems thinking. Using systems thinking, an operations problem within an organization requires understanding how the organization's external environment may have helped shape that problem. We recall from Russ's seminars that he often noted how changing conditions at or outside an organization's boundaries can solve internal operating problems. A high-cost production scheduling problem inside a plant can, in Russ's way of thinking, potentially be better solved by changing the types of customers and their incentives for ordering, rather than the production process itself.

Unlike the mechanistic models that dominated the earlier Industrial Age, systems theory views individuals, teams, organizations, and their operating environments, which we are calling ecosystems, as a dynamic and interdependent whole. Machine Age thinking was literally a product of the Industrial Revolution and viewed the organization as an independent and nearly free agent, able to act on its larger environment and insulated from regulation and control. For individuals, this assumption was manifested in the work of Frederick Taylor (1911) and the Scientific Management movement that broke jobs down into the simplest discrete parts. At an ecosystem level, it freed organizations from concern about their impact on society and the natural environment. Concerns such as the downstream effects of industrial waste in rivers were irrelevant because the impacts were "externalities."

Systems thinking recognizes interdependence as a basic feature of all relationships. Interdependence means that a change in one part of a system implies changes for all other parts of the system; all parts are constantly adjusting to each other. Systems thinking has been manifested in many management fields. When researchers at the Tavistock Institute in London developed "socio-technical systems" design principles in the 1960s through 1970s, individual jobs began to be seen in the context of the work team and the technical systems used to perform them (Herbst, 1974; Trist, Emery, & Murray, 1996). The requirements of the technical and social parts of a system need to be "jointly optimized"—that is, change the technical system and you need to change the way jobs are designed and performed.

Writ large, such thinking is fundamental to understanding everything from the design of your job to the design of an international financial policy regime. This thinking has certainly altered the way many organizations view their impact on the societies and natural environments in which they operate. Once the role of the organization's larger environment is understood, it is possible to trace how rapid and disruptive change is creating new demands for organizations trying to manage their complex, growing interdependencies. Systems thinking paved the way for a succession of new perspectives on organization effectiveness and performance.

Early on, contingency theory stressed the importance of the fit or alignment between an organization's strategy and its structure for determining its performance. The organization that achieved the closest fit between its strategy and its design, it was thought, would outperform its competitors. This view led to more than twenty years of breakthrough work in organization design. The fit models proposed by thought leaders such as Jay Galbraith (1995) and David Nadler (1992), and consulting firms such as McKinsey with its 7-S Model (Peters and Waterman, 1982), all extended our thinking about how to best align the parts of an organization to best execute strategy.

Systems thinking was also showing up in other areas such as leadership theory, where the analog to contingency theory was situational leadership—the idea that the most effective leadership style depended on the situation or context. Similarly, the organization development (OD) movement of the 1960s and 1970s depended on systems models for identifying developmental problems and intervention points for creating change. It was the OD movement that first identified the organization's culture—its values and belief system—as a key target for change. And, of course, the systematic approaches associated with the continuous improvement movement—Total Quality Management (TQM), business process reengineering, Six Sigma, and Lean Design—all had a profound impact on management thinking and organization performance.

It was Michael Porter's groundbreaking industry dynamics model that helped capture specific characteristics of business environments that could be shaped through competitive strategies (Porter, 1980). Similar to the concepts of ecological niche and specialization, the concepts of competitive advantage and distinctive competence became powerful tools for explaining that some organizations outperform others because of their unique assets or alignment with their markets. It is a "positioning" logic.

Later researchers modified the equation to a "resource-based" logic. That is, the unique resources of an organization (Barney, 1991), its capacity for innovation, and stock of intellectual and human capital have all been intensely studied as performance drivers. Moreover, and even more challenging, those special resources came to be seen as "dynamic capabilities" (Eisenhardt & Martin, 2000; Teece, 2007) that need to evolve with the changing environment and with competitors' efforts.

We continue to search for unique organization capabilities, and agility and resiliency are among these. Chapters Three and Six delve deeply into the dynamic capabilities perspective. There we offer what we believe to be a unique framework called "adaptive design," which calls for rethinking organization design in dynamic terms—as a verb, not a noun. For us, adaptive design thinking or a design mindset calls for an active, continuous process of identifying, developing, bundling, and applying capabilities to meet emerging environmental opportunities and challenges. A design mindset grounded in a dynamic capabilities framework is the basis for developing High AR.

Given the continuous need to develop new resources and capabilities to keep an organization aligned with its environment, a powerful shift in focus also occurred when organizations began being viewed as learning systems (Argyris & Schön, 1978; Davenport & Prusak, 1998; de Geus, 1997). Organizational learning (OL) is inherently grounded in systems thinking, but applying human learning concepts based in cognitive psychology to organization-level systems and processes is a challenging task.

Sophisticated and broadly deployed processes, systems, and technologies for acquiring, sharing, retaining, and applying knowledge have emerged to make this happen. From a knowledge management (KM) perspective, high-performing organizations promote individual and team learning through management practices that capture, amplify, move, and apply knowledge to critical knowledge gaps and performance challenges (McCann & Buckner, 2004). Today, KM remains one of the least understood but most critical advances in management thinking and practice. It is a central concept in this book, as later chapters reveal, because OL and KM enable the matching of an organization's environment to its adaptive strategies.

The Changing Nature of Change

There has been a marked shift during this fifty-year time span from viewing organizations as relatively difficult to change structurally to being dynamic and open entities, with every part of them malleable and in constant interaction with their environments. Systems thinking also helped us realize that organizational environments were becoming increasingly turbulent as the global pace of technological change and interdependencies among organizations rapidly accelerated.

Although academics still argue over the best way to measure the dynamics and pace of this change, the basic nature of organizational environments has generally been recognized as rapidly shifting. Managing the environment, regardless of the management theory or model being used, was becoming increasingly difficult. Competitive advantages and distinctive competencies, regardless of the size of investment made to acquire them, were becoming transitory and impossible to sustain.

As Emery and Trist (1965) noted nearly fifty years ago, the basic nature of change was changing. To appreciate the importance of that observation, think about change occurring in essentially three ways over this time period: episodic change, continuous change, and disruptive change. Figure 2.1 illustrates the differences among the three.

Managing Episodic Change

Change was once thought of in episodic terms. Normal, routine operations were interrupted by periods of relatively low-level, manageable disturbances, such as a new product rollout timed for internal operating convenience or a carefully crafted merger. Life cycles of products in markets were measured in years, if not decades. The growth of conglomerate forms of organization through acquisitions was a way of diversifying financial risk and smoothing uncertainty.

The organization's primary objective in this model was to plan and control change to protect the core business. Any unplanned events or changes could be managed by built-in redundancies and slack resources—extra inventory, staff, or money stashed in operating unit budgets—that would serve as buffers to "normalize" operating routines. Strategic planning, as one result, called for linear projections of growth and performance. Heavy regulation

Figure 2.1. The Changing Nature of Change

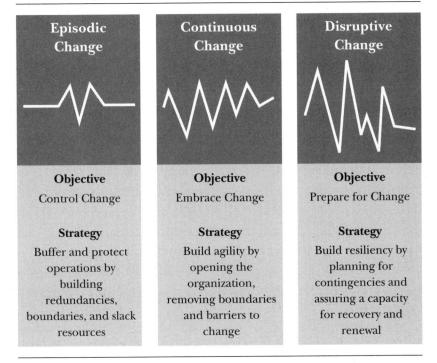

Episodic Change	Continuous Change	Disruptive Change
Objective	**Objective**	**Objective**
Control Change	Embrace Change	Prepare for Change
Strategy	**Strategy**	**Strategy**
Buffer and protect operations by building redundancies, boundaries, and slack resources	Build agility by opening the organization, removing boundaries and barriers to change	Build resiliency by planning for contingencies and assuring a capacity for recovery and renewal

Source: McCann, 2004.

in many industries such as transportation and health care also kept the institutional playing field from changing rapidly, and lobbyists made sure there was home field advantage.

Managing Continuous Change

Organizations continued to induce much greater rates of change through their own competitive dynamics and continuous technological innovation. Institutional barriers were also falling as deregulation spread and new international competitors entered previously secure markets. There were fewer periods of relative calm, and traditional buffers of redundancies and slack resources were driven out by the relentless push for lower costs and an intense business performance focus.

Off-shoring and outsourcing began in earnest and continues to be one outcome in the process of adapting to new global realities. What was occurring in outsourcing from an organization design perspective, of course, was the externalization of interdependencies that previously had been internalized within the organization. Organizations were increasingly opening themselves to their larger environments. In reality, the nature of the costs associated with managing interdependencies had changed, not totally eliminated, and the business focus had shifted from operations inside to those now outside the organization. Organizations had evolved sophisticated controls such as hierarchies for dealing with internal interdependencies among functional areas, but those do not work as well or at all for externalized interdependencies that require continuous monitoring and renegotiation.

Organizations were creating vast new linkages and mutual dependencies, giving rise to new forms of organization that defied ready description and effective management—"network," "virtual," and "boundaryless" as examples (Nadler, 1992). The performance management challenge was escalating to a higher level of analysis where success or failure was based on the performance of an entire set of interdependent organizations such as that in a global supply chain. Jack Welch, former CEO of General Electric, was quoted at the height of this wave of thinking, in Larry Hirschhorn and Tom Gilmore's article "The New Boundaries of the 'Boundaryless' Company": "Our dream for the 1990s is a boundaryless company . . . where we knock down the walls that separate us from each other on the inside and from our key constituencies on the outside" (Hirschhorn & Gilmore, 1992, p. 104).

It was the beginning of what Henry Chesbrough (2003) and others called "The Era of Open Innovation," in which traditional drawings of organizations that showed a solid line between the organization and what was "outside," were now showing dotted lines; boundaries were permeable. Not just open, but *bad*. The argument was that structures and processes, including the cultural values, beliefs, and behaviors that underlie them, can act to slow response time and therefore need to be eliminated or reduced at every opportunity. This meant creating bigger jobs with fewer people, eliminating entire functional groups, reducing layers of management, combining business units, recruiting more talent externally to provide fresh thinking, and relentlessly searching for ways to streamline and speed cycle times. We call this push toward the destruction and elimination of internal and external boundaries the "dominant logic of open organization thinking" (McCann, 2004).

And this is when the race for agility began in earnest. The only choice for organizations experiencing a more rapid pace of change, which they themselves were helping accelerate, was to embrace change—go with it, even accelerate the pace of that change to gain advantage over others moving more slowly. Those that changed slowly or made mistakes in products or markets either underperformed or failed. The challenge was to develop larger global scale while keeping the organization as agile as possible. They chose to do this by opening their boundaries through outsourcing, off-shoring, global expansion, joint ventures, alliances, and other forms of multientity collaboration.

For those with highly developed requisite skills, hypercompetitive or high velocity markets provide opportunities for growth. Many of today's business success stories such as Microsoft, Apple, Oracle, and Intel are based on the abilities of those organizations to change continuously. Andy Grove, for example, honed Intel's capacity for inducing rapid change in the semiconductor industry to a point where he declared: "So give me a turbulent world compared to a stable world and I want the turbulent world" (Karlgaard & Gilder, 1996). Well and good . . . as long as you have developed the adaptive capacity to play that game. Electing to run the fast race without consistently flawless execution meant forsaking market leadership, as Chrysler, Sony, Toyota, and others found. For Enron, it was fatal; for AIG it was a near-death experience (Kansas, 2009; McLean & Elkind, 2003).

Managing Disruptive Change

Continuous change is now a reality for most organizations, but the emerging challenge is also to manage disruptive change. While fast change is challenging, it still can be managed. Savvy firms know the rhythm of new product introductions and industry cycles and build capabilities for managing them. However, it is no longer just the pace of change but the disruptiveness of that change that now demands attention; there are "black swan" events that need to be accounted for, but are almost impossible to anticipate (Taleb, 2007).

Rapid change can at least be anticipated, such as improvements in computing speed or capacity, but severe shocks and surprises such as that of 9/11 can destabilize entire industries and economies in a matter of hours and days. Disruptive change is characterized by periods of sharp, novel conditions from unanticipated sources with debilitating force that upset competitive dynamics and threaten survival (Christensen & Overdorf, 2000; Meyer, 1982; Perrow, 1984). For example, in the past decade the U.S. airline, health care, and financial services industries have faced high levels of disruptive change and their fragility in some cases has become all too apparent (Kansas, 2009; Meyer, Goes, & Brooks, 1993). Weaknesses in a system are quickly revealed as the shocks are transmitted through underappreciated or undermanaged interdependencies in information systems, power grids, and transportation networks. Some boundaries, whether geographical or regulatory, that once provided time and space between organizations have been eliminated.

Working at and Beyond Capacity

There are absolutely wonderful benefits that accrue to organizations that open themselves to new and valuable relationships with other organizations and embrace the change that such relationships induce. Organizations learn from each other, streamline their operations by sharing costs and responsibilities, and expand their market presence. Today's global supply chains in the clothing, electronics, and automobile industries, and the value creation networks among biotech/pharmaceutical companies, are clear examples of such benefits.

Openness is not cost or risk free, however. An organization's performance critically depends on its effective development and deployment of the requisite skills for operating in dynamic, open organizational environments on a global scale. Figure 2.2

Figure 2.2. Benefits of Openness Relative to Adaptive Capacity Investment

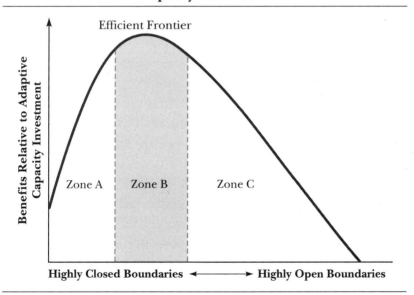

Source: McCann, 2004.

illustrates what happens when the benefits of greater openness are traded off against the costs and risks associated with managing the greater number and intensity of interdependencies and risks posed by those relationships.

It is the creation and effective deployment of sufficient adaptive capacity that mediates that trade-off. In Zone A the benefits of increasing openness greatly exceed the costs and risks, and the organization's adaptive capacity for managing those relationships is more than adequate. The organization in Zone A can benefit from more openness through even more external relationships that create additional value. For example, a European telecommunications company could outsource its engineering services to a provider in Bangalore, India, as long as the company is prepared to manage that new relationship to sustain high support levels. For example, training its engineers in cross-cultural project management and investing in videoconferencing capabilities to facilitate interactions would be essential, to say the least.

In Zone B, all of the relationships and interdependencies created demand the total commitment of the organization's adaptive capacity. All benefits are being optimized and only the additional investments of capacity—more staff, bigger budgets, and even better communications technologies—would allow further expansion of external relationships. The right people with the right skills and capabilities, financial resources, and technologies must be in place and sustained if the organization is to stay at that ideal zone on the curve. Conditions always change, however, whether with external service providers or disruptions in supply chains. Just because something is working really well doesn't mean that additional investments aren't necessary to sustain that performance as conditions change. We can all describe examples of initiatives that have had resources reduced to the point that they are no longer sustained at needed levels. The challenge is to continuously monitor and manage the demands posed by all those interdependencies and then ensure that you are investing in the capacity to meet those demands.

When those investments are not made quickly enough or sustained, a tipping point is reached and the organization enters Zone C, where capacity demands for managing its relationships (staff, time, budgets) now exceed the organization's actual investments in them. At that point, the organization becomes overexposed to its relationships. The relationships are being undermanaged. The costs and risks are thus exceeding the benefits gained and downside risks are increased. The organization is now on the way to becoming fragile in the sense that disruptive shocks experienced through its relationship partners can now damage its own performance. How severe will be unknown and depend on what surprises the environment brings and how quickly these are imported into the organization through its relationships.

Unfortunately, fragility is at times revealed only after a surprise or shock when the organization has to act in unanticipated ways, such as during the financial system near-collapse of 2008 and the 2011 Fukushima nuclear disaster. Numerous examples of Zone C organizations can be found, but the M&A waves of the 1980s and 1990s provide far too many cases of companies like AT&T, Nortel, Lucent Technologies, Enron, and WorldCom, which simply could not manage what they created—levels of complexity and change through dozens of rapid acquisitions and underfunded integration programs. Enron and WorldCom had other huge issues, of course, but they were definitely not adept at managing the complexity that they created for themselves, thus complicating matters even more. These companies created seriously undermanaged relationships with others that simply couldn't be managed well when the economy shifted or one of the acquisitions failed.

The outsourcing movement that started in the past decade is similarly now encountering the hidden costs and risks associated with externalized and undermanaged interdependencies in global supply chains (Barthelemy, 2003). As a result, companies in the United States and Europe are near-shoring or returning to their home countries entire operations drawn away by the promise of low-cost labor.

Are the consequences of failing to build sufficient adaptive capacity for prevailing conditions always sudden and fatal, as the above examples might suggest? Not at all. There are degrees of performance degradation, as suggested in Chapter One. As an organization-level extreme case, an organization may totally and suddenly collapse, resulting in a bankruptcy and take-over like that experienced by the total collapse of Lehman Brothers and last-minute rescue of Merrill Lynch in a shotgun marriage to Bank of America. Both caused extensive additional collateral damage to the entire financial ecosystem. How extensive that damage may be depends on the agility and resilience of those other interdependent organizations, but this example is decidedly the extreme case.

Less extreme, an organization may completely fail without major ecosystem ripple effects; it simply disappears from a crowded marketplace almost without anyone noticing except perhaps stockholders and employees. This often happens in the retail sector, as in the case of Circuit City or Borders. An organization may also survive a shock or serious disruption, but have its performance so debilitated that it is susceptible to another shock or surprise. Its immune system had been weakened. Such is the case with Toyota Motor Company after its 2007 U.S. auto recalls, followed too closely by the 2011 Japanese earthquake and tsunami. Toyota moved from first to third place in worldwide auto production market share as a result. It may recover market share, but the costs of doing so are tremendous.

Can the same curvilinear model in Figure 2.2 be applied to an ecosystem, individual, and team? Absolutely yes! There are many such examples of movements into zone C in the airline, automotive, and financial sectors. We will discuss many of these over the next chapters to illustrate specific adaptive capacity flaws that led to their near collapses.

Likewise, individuals also benefit from greater openness and engagement with others. We all know individuals who overextend, overcommit, and overpromise. The resulting stress, anxiety, and crazy work pace lead to their illness, to seriously dysfunctional behaviors, and certainly to burnouts, meltdowns, career derailments, and even deaths.

The same dynamic works for teams because team performance is so much a function of individual team member performance. When one or more individual team members can no longer sustain the pace and disruptiveness of change, then team performance suffers. More than one M&A team has had a key team member succumb to the grueling pace of a drawn-out merger negotiation and integration process. We will have much more to say about individual- and team-level consequences of turbulence in Chapter Four.

Summary

If we are indeed entering a period of more disruptive change, along with rapid continuous change, then the repertoire of adaptive strategies and capabilities has to be quickly expanded. If the objective during episodic change is to control it, and the objective during rapid change is to embrace it, then the objective during disruptive change is to prepare for it. The message from Figure 2.2 is that some organizations suffer while others can prosper, as long as they develop the capacity needed to match the conditions they encounter and create. Chapter Three provides the understanding and tools for helping you do precisely that for your own organization.

chapter
THREE

Not *A*, Not *R*—It's *AR*

Chapter Two provided you with a broad perspective on how we think turbulence has become endemic, how its consequences pose critical challenges, and how managing turbulence sometimes calls for counterintuitive actions. We did our best to make concepts and ideas accessible by providing a historical and conceptual foundation for understanding how we have now arrived at this point. Unfortunately, the management literature regarding environmental turbulence is still just too academic to be of practical help. While we academics argue among ourselves about how to best *measure* turbulence, the conditions facing all of us certainly *feel* turbulent.

The argument advanced in Chapters One and Two makes the case that rapid, disruptive change is increasing turbulence so much that it threatens to overwhelm our adaptive capacities. However, turbulence is being experienced unevenly because adaptive capacities vary tremendously from individual to individual, team to team, and organization to organization. Each of us may exacerbate turbulence through our own unilateral actions, then find it difficult, if not impossible, to manage what we helped create. This is a bit like Mickey Mouse as the Sorcerer's Apprentice in Disney's *Fantasia*—he was great at getting something started but ended up flooding the castle.

The trade-off is not just managing rapid change or just managing disruptive change. We live in a time when both are essential simultaneously. Table 3.1 summarizes the argument that it is not *either/or* but *both/and* when it comes to meeting the challenge of turbulence. We have all witnessed cases of organizations trying to change quickly, often too quickly, to match the pace of change in an industry, only to lose control of operations and finances and then crash; such organizations were built for speed, not endurance. The challenge is to build organizations that are fast and flexible, but at the same time able to weather setbacks and surprises.

Mastering increasing turbulence also requires building the right kind and amount of adaptive capacity, at least at the same pace that turbulence accelerates. That was the message from Figure 2.2 in the previous chapter. Investing in the skills and capabilities for keeping up with the growing complexity and operating scale of your organization sounds right, but adaptive capacity is a difficult concept to capture and operationalize. We think of

Table 3.1. The Challenge of Managing Rapid and Disruptive Change

Both:	And:
• Managing the Rate of Change	• Managing Disruptive Change
• Encouraging Interdependence	• Encouraging Independence
• Creating Rapid Growth	• Creating Sustainable Growth
• Designing Large Scale	• Designing Manageable Scale
• Building Agility	• Building Resiliency

adaptive capacity in terms of two critical, more specific capacities—agility and resiliency.

A Race for Agility and Quest for Resiliency

Agility and resiliency are not new concepts. They have been receiving greater attention recently for obvious reasons; they are believed essential for managing turbulent change. However, these concepts are themselves complex and difficult to put to work effectively. The literature around them is messy and confusing; the concepts are not defined well and are often used interchangeably. Perhaps most important, they are rarely considered together. It was not until our 2006 AMA/HRI research that these concepts had even been empirically tested together for their relationship to organization performance (McCann, Selsky, & Lee, 2009).

Prescriptions for building agility and resiliency require caveats, just like you see in a magazine advertisement for a prescription drug. Chapter Two described, for example, how the "race for agility" is a response by organizations to the increasing pace of change and clamorous calls for ever greater speed to match that pace of change. This is a dangerous race, as it can destroy valuable buffers and boundaries, lean the organization too much (as Toyota Motor Company reportedly found in 2009 with its massive recalls), or create unrecognized and undermanaged interdependencies, like those revealed in the financial services sector in 2008 when it was impossible to decipher what exactly was contained in globally traded bundles of toxic assets. The real danger is that those undermanaged relationships can create excessive risks—just as the number of serious external shocks and surprises is also increasing.

As a result, the race for agility instead often creates *fragility*—individuals, teams, and organizations that break far too readily as operating conditions intensify beyond their adaptive capacity. They simply do not build and sustain sufficient adaptive capacity to manage the complexity they create and are then over-exposed to their environments. This concept is more than just a metaphor. Individuals may break when they become more susceptible to mental and physical collapse due to sustained high levels of anxiety and stress, or they can simply disengage or exit a crazy work environment in an organization that is not managing turbulence well.

Teams may break due to excessive member turnover or work demands that simply cannot be met with the resources provided. Organizations may break when overwhelmed by a natural disaster, such as Tokyo Electric Power Company at Fukushima, which was further compounded by inadequate risk management practices. More typically, fragility is expressed as increasingly slow responses to situations, empty new-product pipelines, or high turnover in the top management team. Entire ecosystems may break, as in the airline industry after 9/11 or the global financial services system in 2008. Fortunately, most of these can be repaired, but how quickly and effectively depends on just how agile and resilient they may be.

This is one reason why the "quest for resilience," as Gary Hamel and Liisa Välikangas (2003) call it, has now become so important. They noted, "Call it the resilience gap. The world is becoming turbulent faster than organizations are becoming resilient" (Hamel and Välikangas, 2003, p. 1). Like agility, resiliency is also a more complicated concept than meets the eye. For example, we all can think of resilient individuals who coped with personal setbacks such as financial ruin or poor health but later went on to success. Diane Coutu (2002) even stressed, "More than education, more than experience, more than training, a person's level of resilience will determine who succeeds and who fails. That's true in the cancer ward, it's true in the Olympics, and it's true in the boardroom" (Coutu, 2002, p. 48).

Yet to talk about a resilient team or organization or ecosystem in the same way is a stretch. Are the same psychological, physical, and emotional characteristics and capabilities ascribed to resilient individuals really appropriate for describing resilient teams and organizations? Well, yes and no, actually; we have found that some aspects of agility and resiliency are indeed similar whereas others are very different across those levels of analysis.

Although the interest in agility and resiliency is understandable, it is curious that the two concepts have rarely been considered together. Our research found that their separate treatment creates seriously misleading action implications. It may be easy for you to think of agility as a capacity for managing rapid change, and of resiliency as a capacity for managing disruptive change. That is too easy. Their relationships are actually much more intertwined; moving aggressively in building one without attention to the other in turbulent environments can cause damage. What we have found in our research is that they are empirically distinct, with each capturing something different about adaptive capacity, yet still highly correlated concepts.

Indeed, we want to make a case that it is not just agility (A), and it is not just resiliency (R)—it is agility *and* resiliency (AR)—that is needed for building adaptive capacity. They are two distinct concepts yet they should be thought of as two sides of the single coin called adaptive capacity. We refer to their highly correlated, synergistic relationship as "AR" from this point forward.

Building AR at Four Levels

Although our focus is essentially at the level of your organization, we are equally concerned about how individuals like yourself and the teams in which you participate contribute to organization-level adaptive capacity. We believe a focus on individuals and teams is absolutely essential because the consequences of increasing turbulence play out just as intensely at those two levels as at an organization level. Indeed, in a later chapter we discuss how individuals and teams actually bear the brunt of poor turbulence management at the organization level. It is impossible for an organization to achieve sustainable high performance when its individuals and teams are struggling and not managing excessive change well.

Despite the usual joking about ineffective committees and task forces, the reality is that teams and groups are the basic organization design element for getting things done in all modern organizations—when they work well, that is. Teams are only as good as the individuals within them, and there is little question that individual performance contributes to organization performance, but individual effort is most often leveraged through others.

In addition, we believe that organizations must also work more effectively at a higher level—their ecosystems. Following past usage in *Harvard Business Review* and elsewhere, we will call this the ecosystem level (Iansiti & Levien, 2004). This is a big step up in thinking about how organizations manage turbulence and therefore requires explanation. The ecosystem is where the single organization becomes part of multiple larger sets of organizations and groups, all linked through shared interests, goals, or geography. An organization may be a member of an industry association, a key or peripheral player in a public policy sector such as health care, a dominant competitor that sets conditions for others in a regional marketplace, or a vital institution in a local community where its production facilities lie.

Those identities, and the interorganizational relationships among the various other players, pose contingencies and risks that must be managed mindfully and strategically. *Strategic boundary management* is what we call attention to such relationships; that is, relationships are systematically created when potentially valuable, sustained when currently useful, or eliminated when the risks and costs associated with them become excessive. Strategic boundary management may well be one of the highest priorities and skills for managing disruptive environments.

An organization may pursue its interests through others, but it is the interdependencies built among members of that larger ecosystem that become the transmitters of change and disruption into organizations. The ecosystem is where collective strategies and collaborative networks come into play. Therefore, the objectives at this level are to create a sense of shared identity and fate, and then to establish more defensible, less turbulent operating space by collaboratively engaging others in managing the turbulence everyone shares.

The organization's mission is therefore complex. It has to manage turbulence *down, around,* and *up. Down* for its individuals and teams, *across* all its operations and functions, and *up* in its relationships with other organizations and groups that compose its ecosystems. Only when all three of these other levels are actively and effectively developed and sustained in their agility and resiliency can any organization master turbulence.

Five High AR Capabilities

We have identified five critical capabilities of High AR individuals, teams, organizations, and ecosystems. All five have been found across a wide variety of organizational settings. Some were initially identified and defined through large interactive workshops with senior HR executives in the United States, Canada, and England, and others in our global AMA/HRI survey and subsequent empirical research.

Many organizations are doing excellent work in building these capabilities under a variety of names and for many reasons. We have spoken to executives within many of these organizations, and they provided us with case studies and examples of their experiences, many of which we recount in this book. However, our work is still in a nascent stage and there are likely, almost certainly, additional capabilities beyond the five we have identified. We think these five provide a very important start.

Each of these five capabilities has an extensive theoretical pedigree derived from multiple fields of study, such as management, psychology and the biosciences. Our goal here is to create clarity for operating managers by translating the capabilities for action. At the risk of advancing what sounds like truisms or creating oversimplifications that mask their rich theoretical heritages, we believe that High AR individuals, teams, organizations, and ecosystems are: Being Purposeful, Being Aware, Being Action-Oriented, Being Resourceful, and Being Networked. Table 3.2 (on pages 44 and 45) outlines the full model and shows how these capabilities are expressed across the four levels.

This is a formidable model to absorb all at once, and we devote a full chapter to each of the five capabilities to examine their full potential. However, as a preview of those chapters and to provide you with a guide to this model, each of the capabilities is briefly described next. We suggest reading the table horizontally, taking each capability across the individual, team, organization, and ecosystem levels. The levels support each other and each provides the context for the others.

Being Purposeful

High AR individuals, teams, organizations, and ecosystems cultivate positive identities grounded in a core set of values and beliefs about who they are and what they want to accomplish. They seek "wellness"—a quality that we think of as a healthy physical, psychological, and social life that supports their sustained pursuit of that purpose.

At an individual level, being purposeful means that you maintain a positive self-concept and a physically and psychologically healthy presence. These are capable of sustaining you in highly ambiguous, stressful, and demanding work situations. With High AR Purpose, you also develop and maintain positive relationships with others at work, in your family and personal relationships, in your community, and in the larger world by staying in touch with what is happening to others elsewhere. These relationships become extremely important when conditions become most demanding.

At a team level, individual members have shared values and beliefs that support their collaborative work performance. Their values and beliefs are aligned and resonant in such a way that they draw strength and vitality from each other. No single individual drags down the team's ability to achieve its work goals because of a lack of wellness.

At the organization level, the leadership team vividly and frequently communicates and manifests the organization's set of shared values/beliefs within a compelling vision and sustainable concept of the organization within society. Stephen R. Covey calls this the organization's "significant contribution" (2004) and it is essential for employee engagement and self-fulfillment. The organization expresses sincere commitment and support for wellness initiatives as one aspect of its pursuit for continuous improvement.

For the ecosystem, purposefulness exists when a group of organizations share the belief that their collective efforts yield valuable contributions to each other, the economy, and society. As a result, there is a strong, shared sense of legitimacy among its members and stakeholders that affirms their collective sense of purpose and meaning. They create what Porter and Kramer (2011) call "shared value" for themselves and for society. Industry groups such as health care networks, humanitarian associations, and certain kinds of cross-sector social partnerships are examples (Selsky & Parker, 2010).

Being Aware

High AR individuals, teams, organizations, and ecosystems are aware of their larger environment, actively scan and engage in

Table 3.2. Five AR Capabilities Across Levels

Capacity	Level			
	Individual	Team	Organization	Ecosystem
Being Purposeful Holding positive, "well" identities grounded in core values and beliefs about who they are and want to be	Positive self-concept with a physically and psychologically healthy presence capable of sustaining them in highly ambiguous, stressful work situations	Shared values and beliefs supporting collaborative performance, with no one compromised in psychological and physical fitness to limit team performance	Vivid, frequently communicated, and manifested shared values/beliefs within a compelling vision and sustainable concept of the organization within society	Shared beliefs that collaborative efforts yield valued economic and social contributions, supporting a sense of legitimacy, purpose, and meaning
Being Aware Aware of the larger environment, actively scanning and engaging in sensemaking to form action hypotheses	Active learners with a curiosity about the larger world, open to change and able to make sense and act in ambiguous environments	Well-developed information gathering, filtering, sharing, and decision-making processes supporting collective sensemaking	Formalized and fully supported strategic knowledge management (KM) roles and processes linked to key decision makers	Widely shared information and support for specialized sensemaking, and for interpretation functions

Being Action-Oriented Forward-leaning and open to change, with appropriate tools for quick movement, proactively or reactively, alone or collaboratively	Confident and competent in taking the initiative, acting or reacting as necessary, to gain advantage, avoid collisions, or minimize setbacks	Shared problem-solving, decision-making, and implementation skills, empowered by key decision makers to act and react quickly	Engaged in strategic boundary management to create, sustain, or destroy barriers to action using a broad array of strategies, tools, and processes	Shared appreciation of a situation and a developed capacity for broad-based collaborative action for sustained impact
Being Resourceful Creatively and innovatively using resources with the capacity and skills to attract additional resources as needed	Entrepreneurial in securing resources, talent, and support required to meet a goal, despite setbacks	Well-developed practices and processes that bring out the best thinking and innovative ideas from team members and team supporters	Creative and innovative in how it develops and uses scarce or valuable resources—financial, physical, and human	Highly developed processes for attracting, mobilizing, and sharing resources from within or outside the group
Being Networked Building and sustaining valued relationships for leveraging opportunity or support when overwhelmed, eliminating the ones posing excessive risks	Positive, active relationships maintained within the immediate family, work group, and community to sustain a sense of connectedness and meaning	Supportive relationships among its own members and other parts of the organization, and tightly integrated into the core functioning of the organization	Actively managed relationship networks supported across the organization and with external organizations and groups important to its performance	Collectively maintained and supported relationships, even governing units to manage member relationships, with active linkages to other ecosystems for shared responses

sensemaking of what they perceive and experience, and are able to form action hypotheses about the opportunities and risks detected. They are active learners and open to new ideas to improve their performance. They are not reluctant to experiment with ideas or processes that may be contrary to prevailing wisdom or practice. Because they effectively work at making sense of events in uncertain, ambiguous conditions, they have the ability to operate more effectively.

These qualities also readily apply for individuals like yourself, but we know that expecting open-mindedness and heightened awareness among distressed, information-overloaded individuals is counterintuitive. The natural reaction is to withdraw, not open up to even more information, ambiguity and uncertainty; this is called the "threat-rigidity effect" (Staw, Sandelands, & Dutton, 1981). Nonetheless, High AR Aware individuals have a finely tuned capacity for sensemaking and acting on their environments for their benefit. They are active learners with a curiosity about the larger world, able to place events in context and with sufficient meaning to act or react.

Being aware at a team level means having well-developed information gathering, filtering, sharing, and group decision-making processes that support collective sensemaking and creation of action hypotheses to guide action. These processes may be parts of routines and protocols they've informally developed, or parts of sophisticated technologies and information system platforms that all can access and use. With the communication technologies available today, they are often team members spread around the world.

Such systems and processes, along with highly developed roles and specialized responsibilities, become even more formalized and broadly based at the organization level. Ready examples include strategic planning and scenario building processes and practices, or competitive intelligence units that are constantly scanning and interpreting what is happening outside the organization. Scenario-based planning (discussed in more detail in Chapter Five) may be used at that level, for example, to test ideas and surface alternative interpretations of the future based on the ideas perceived to be moving in the larger environment.

An example of awareness at the ecosystem level is when organizations share information with each other across an entire value chain to better coordinate their actions. Global supply chain members collaborate continuously to wring costs out of products and manage supply. Industry associations or specialized research groups such as i4cp in the HR domain or Gartner in the IT domain also perform invaluable scanning, sensemaking, and interpretation functions for ecosystem members.

Being Action-Oriented

Being High AR Action-Oriented means having a "forward-leaning" posture and an openness to change made possible with access to appropriate resources—people, systems, processes, and structures —for supporting quick movement, whether proactively or reactively. Action-oriented individuals, teams, organizations, and ecosystems are capable of intelligently acting alone or in collaboration with others. They are strongly predisposed toward execution, which is reinforced and supported by those resources.

At the individual level, this means that you would feel confident and competent in taking the initiative, preparing and acting, or reacting as necessary, to create an advantage or avoid a collision with an event. This is hardly a headlong rush toward frivolous action. Action is premeditated and calculated, with full recognition and anticipation of both the upside potential and downside risks associated with acting quickly and decisively.

Although an individual may be a powerful actor, able to decisively affect a situation facing the organization, such instances are actually relatively rare. It is the team that is usually the basic unit of analysis and device for executing change. This may be a work team on the shop floor or a C-suite executive team. For your team, this means having the shared, highly developed problem-solving, decision-making, and implementation skills for quickly deploying and redeploying all necessary resources. The team must have access to key decision makers and be empowered to act and react quickly and decisively enough to preserve advantage. Though each team member may bring unique skills to the group, your critical challenge is to make sure that team performance is never damaged by weaknesses in individual team members and changes in team membership. Members are cross-trained and ambidextrous, and smoothly introduced and exited because teaming routines and competencies are highly valued and developed.

For the organization, it must create an adaptive design mindset that fundamentally alters how an organization's design and structure are visualized. An organization design is an expression of the preferred choice for adapting the organization to a chosen environment for greatest impact through its goal-seeking strategies. We give names to those common organization designs, such as functional, business divisional, matrix, and so on, and we design individual jobs and teams with the same objective in mind—thus grouping or bundling tasks into discrete units (jobs, teams, divisions, and so forth) in the most efficient and effective ways. We create structure once we give those units names and portray their relationships to each other using boxes linked by lines on a chart.

As Chapter Six will stress, however, we also think of structure as recurring, interdependent relationships among capabilities that are grouped and bundled together to support specific goals and strategies. We think that managers have in the past seriously overfocused on structure as static, rather than dynamic, patterns of relationships. In our view, structure is an expression of how specific sets of capabilities are grouped or bundled at a moment in time.

AR is a bundle of capabilities—we've identified our five—that are thoughtfully and systematically developed and applied to quickly and decisively master knowledge gaps between the organization's current capabilities and what its environment is presenting. Being High AR Action-Oriented at the organization level means finely tuning the process of identifying needed capabilities, developing and bundling them, and then applying them for maximum impact.

At an ecosystem level, collective action becomes more challenging because each organization has its own drive for survival, and they all have greatly varying capabilities for moving quickly and sustainably as turbulence increases. Central to ecosystem-level action is a *shared* appreciation of what is happening in the arena of common interest, including the advantages of collective action or the consequences of inaction—in other words, a sense of shared fate and desirable outcome exists (McCann, 1983; Normann & Ramirez, 1993; Selsky & McCann, 2008). We emphasize the word shared because it will be impossible to build High AR at that level without that sense of shared predicament, fate, and future as a foundation for collective action.

Ideally, there will be institutional or agreed-upon mechanisms for building a shared appreciation and supporting communication, mobilization, and coordinated, sustained action across all ecosystem members. Lobbying efforts by trade associations and interest groups, for example, are immensely effective at enabling or blocking public policy initiatives. NGO networks are also able to mobilize swiftly and deploy tremendous amounts of humanitarian resources during disasters such as the earthquakes in Haiti or Japan. The Occupy movements in various cities across the United States in late 2011 are examples of collaborative action that were not able to be uniformly sustained because they lacked several essential competencies, skills, and resources associated with High AR.

Learning how to strategically manage boundaries shared with others is an essential part of being High AR Action-Oriented.

If all of the relationships in ecosystems pose opportunities for collaborative action on shared issues, they also pose significant risks, as illustrated in Figure 2.2. We believe that many individuals, teams, organizations, and entire ecosystems are dangerously over-connected and that greater selectivity in who and how we interact with others is necessary. We spend a substantial part of Chapter Six discussing why and how strategic boundary management is so critical in turbulent environments.

Being Resourceful

Being High AR Resourceful assumes that organizations have learned how to use different creativity and innovation scripts to exploit opportunities or minimize setbacks. They have highly developed knowledge and skills for attracting, deploying, and redeploying their resources, whether economic, physical, human, or organizational. There are many ways of being resourceful, but in Chapter Seven we try to simplify thinking about this capability by offering four specific "scripts" or approaches to creative and innovative thinking and action.

A resourceful individual behaves much like an entrepreneur engaged in the ongoing quest for the resources, talent, and support required to grow a big idea in spite of setbacks. If you are a highly resourceful individual, then you'll have the predisposition and drive to pursue your big idea and have also acquired the knowledge and skills to do so. Pursuit is thoughtful, planned, and draws on all the talent and resources from whatever source you need to support your effort.

For your team, resourcefulness is expressed through practices and processes that bring out the best thinking and innovative ideas from all team members and others supporting the team. Group development practices designed to enhance team creativity and innovativeness have now become common rituals in most knowledge-based companies. Highly resourceful teams are able to think and act creatively in realizing advantages or minimizing setbacks, but are also adept at attracting, deploying, and redeploying their resources needed as conditions change.

Being Resourceful at the organization level means building an innovating mindset and a culture that sustains it in the midst of turbulent change. Although innovativeness is most often expressed through the introduction of new products and services, it also focuses on the organization's own internal processes and activities; relentless continuous improvement is the norm, not a slogan. The organization is also innovative in how it develops and uses its resources, particularly financial, physical, and human assets. This is a distinguishing feature of High AR organizations, which can take what they have at hand and then reuse it in novel ways to meet novel circumstances. This is the concept of *bricolage*, which we explore in Chapter Seven.

At the ecosystem level, Being Resourceful means that a shared issue or condition will be creatively explored and met with collaborative action. Members craft inventive ways to complement each other's strengths and weaknesses and experiment with ways to accomplish their shared goals together. Mutual assistance is an established practice in a highly resourceful ecosystem because members share a sense of purpose and belief that the continued viability and health of individual members benefits the whole. They may develop elaborate, finely tuned protocols and processes for mobilizing and sharing resources to support each other, or some members may have well-established and reliable access to valuable resources outside the group.

Being Networked

Being Networked for individuals, teams, organizations, and ecosystems means building and sustaining valued relationships that they use for leveraging opportunity and as a lifeline when their own capacity is overwhelmed. They are able to call on their network of relationships when stressed beyond their own ability to act. When those relationships pose excessive risks or costs to sustain, they may end them. Although networked entities prefer to "go it together" rather than "go it alone," they balance the value and risks associated with their relationships.

Being a High AR Networked individual means maintaining positive, active relationships with your immediate family, work group, and larger community. You gain a sense of engagement and meaning through those relationships and are sustained during challenging times by the positive energy and support they provide to you.

A highly networked team sustains positive relationships with other teams and parts of the organization. It is tightly integrated into the functioning of the organization with ready access to key decision makers and the resources needed to act quickly.

At the organization level, relationship networks are supported across all parts and levels of the organization, and with external organizations and groups important to its performance. Those relationships are recognized as critically important to take what Rosabeth Moss Kanter (1994) calls "collaborative advantage" of a situation, or when the organization is severely threatened beyond its own ability to respond and only collective action will do.

Managing networks requires constantly monitoring organizational boundaries and barriers to make sure individuals and teams can work across them to quickly seize opportunities. Conversely, managing networks must minimize the damages of turbulence by creating or sustaining boundaries and barriers—strategic boundary management, in our vocabulary. Global supply chain networks and alliances illustrate how organizations redefine boundaries and create strategies and tools for managing them. When clear advantage or excessive risk is perceived, they may acquire or divest business units to build or contain those networks.

Organizations have a broad and sophisticated array of strategies, tools, and processes for accomplishing this. For example, they may eliminate internal layers of management or units, redesign processes, or create specialized roles and units such as M&A teams to support their actions, with well-rehearsed action scenarios and game plans at hand.

Finally, in High AR Networked ecosystems, members maintain relationships supported by associations or groups, perhaps even establishing governing bodies or groups that manage or regulate member relationships. The well-networked ecosystem is also integrally linked with other networks of organizations in the event that responses to shared situations between ecosystems need to be managed. Ecosystem-level action is evident in the broad-based response to Hurricane Katrina in New Orleans, the responses in many sectors such as airlines and energy to 9/11, or joint actions of the Federal Reserve and other reserve banks to the 2008 financial crisis. These were messy, complicated, protracted, and uneven in impact, but essentially successful in extending boundaries to incorporate all those needed for acting at the scale of the damage.

Bringing It All Together

These five capabilities are relevant across all four of the levels described, and each has core dimensions or characteristics that are manifested in similar and different ways across those levels. When an entity has highly developed one or more of them we will refer to them as a High AR individual, team, or organization. And as we have argued, the organization must be aware of and intervene at the next level up, the business ecosystem, to build agility and resiliency. As you move from the individual to higher levels in Table 3.2, those interventions become increasingly varied and grow in scale and sophistication in terms of the processes, systems, structures, and ways of managing and sustaining them.

AR is without question greatest when these five capabilities are harmonized and aligned across all four levels. For example, AR is greatest when your own core values and beliefs are consonant and aligned across the other three levels. When they are not, performance may be compromised. It is impossible for you to stay in an organization that does not share your values and beliefs or is not making a contribution to society that you accept as important. Individuals leave such organizations, including dysfunctional teams not supported by management. Consider Enron or Lehman Brothers in this respect, as we do in later chapters.

In sum, the leadership challenge we pose for you over the next chapters for building High AR is to:

- Build agility and resiliency together—neither is sufficient, both are essential
- Develop both at multiple levels—individual, team, organization, and ecosystem
- Align and dynamically balance both across these levels as conditions change, through sustained support and strategically designed and managed interventions

We recognize that this is no small challenge for you. In the chapters to follow we try to provide examples of individuals, teams, organizations, and ecosystem-level groups of organizations that demonstrate just how these capabilities can be used to sustain high performance as turbulence accelerates.

chapter
FOUR

Being Well and Acting with Purpose

Purposeful thinking and behaviors are the foundation capability for High AR individuals, teams, and organizations within their ecosystems. Purposefulness—thought and supportive action based on a clear sense of purpose and grounded in a positive self-identity and core set of values and beliefs—is more than goal-seeking behavior. Goals are tools for realizing purpose and will shift, whereas purpose remains nearly constant. Purpose sustains a positive identity regardless what happens, whether in our own personal lives when fired from a job or following the collapse of the South Tower in the World Trade Center if you were a senior partner at Sandler O'Neill & Partners (Freeman, Hirschhorn, & Maltz, 2004; Nocera, 2006).

Purpose serves as a reference point to stabilize and sustain focus, attention, and behavior while responses take shape and recovery occurs. At the extreme, that sense of purpose may have to serve as the bare foundation on which a dramatically transformed new life, organization, or industry is built when your previous one collapses. No better example of this is the U.S. auto industry in the wake of the Great Recession.

This is purposefulness from a *resiliency* perspective, and it is most often tested under hostile conditions. From an *agility* perspective, a well-understood, operationally expressed, and widely shared sense of purpose provides you with a powerful vantage point for acting quickly and proactively in turbulent environments. Such confusing conditions require a firm basis for critical judgments and sound decisions grounded in the core values and beliefs supporting purpose. Agility in terms of purposefulness links cognition with fast, flexible action where values and beliefs filter, screen, and prioritize what is worth pursuing and what is not. Debate is limited to how, not whether, to act.

The wellspring of purposefulness in Western civilization was the ancient Greeks' debates over teleology—purpose that gives things meaning. Since the Enlightenment, moral philosophers, including Hume, William James, and C. S. Pierce, have explored our social nature. Our take on purposefulness follows from what are arguably their descendants, such well-known management authors as Peter Senge (1990, 2010), Jim Collins and Jerry Porras (2002), and Stephen Covey (2004). A slew of other popular authors from Daniel Pink in *Drive: The Surprising Truth about What Motivates Us* (Pink, 2011) to health-minded Robert Rosen at Healthy Companies International (www.healthycompanies.com) also stress the role of purpose.

For us, the contribution of Victor Frankl has always underpinned this perspective. In *Man's Search for Meaning* (1959/1984), Frankl made the case for a core sense of purpose as the foundation for surviving the harshest of all conditions, Nazi concentration camps. Frankl can be misunderstood about what purpose meant to him, instead referring to it, as least as we read it, as a process: "In a position of utter desolation, when man cannot express himself in positive action, when his only achievement may consist in enduring his sufferings in the right way—an honorable way—in such a position man can, through loving contemplation of the image he carries of his beloved, achieve fulfillment" (p. 57). Other authors have viewed purpose more as an objective state. Without referencing Frankl, Senge made the case by noting, "Real vision cannot be understood in isolation from the idea of purpose. By purpose, I mean an individual's sense of why he is alive" (Senge, 1990, p. 148). Similarly, Collins and Porras (2002) stress the fundamental importance of a "core ideology," consisting of core values, core purpose, and an envisioned future as essential for a positive self-identity. Regardless of whether it is a process or a state, purpose is a foundational concept for us.

Purpose as Vision Statement

For organizations, a vision statement, often accompanied by a statement of core values, is its expression of purpose. The vision statement is a relatively new stage in the usual strategic planning process. It arose in the early 1980s when strategy theorists found that starting the process with goals and objectives, as had been done for decades, was not enough to account for strategic success. Tom Peters and Robert Waterman's *In Search of Excellence* (1982) was instrumental in getting visions grafted onto the front end of strategic planning models in most strategy textbooks. Common features of effective vision statements have been distilled over the past two decades and are found in many strategy textbooks. For example, Arthur Thompson, Lonnie Strickland, and John Gamble's popular text *Crafting and Executing Strategy* (2010) indicates that "an effectively worded vision statement should be: graphic, directional, focused, flexible, feasible, desirable and easy to communicate" (Thompson et al., 2010, p. 26).

A good vision statement is much more than sloganeering or the good idea of the month. Vision statements can be exceptionally effective during turbulence when they are prepared thoughtfully and articulated consistently so that everyone understands and embraces them. Better yet, it is even more powerful when people see you living the values espoused in actual practice.

At Southwest Airlines, for example, its early mission statement was developed over thirty years ago and was very specific: Southwest was meant to be a "price competitive, commuter and short-haul airline using close-in airports." This statement was operationally sound but not exactly captivating. More important, though, Southwest wanted "to involve customers and employees in the product and the process, making it a fun, profitable, and quality experience" (H. Putnam, 2009, p.14). They do this better than anyone else in their industry. Simon Sinek used Southwest Airlines to make the point, in his book *Start with Why: How Great Leaders Inspire Everyone to Take Action* (2009), that it isn't *what* you do but *why* you do it that captures hearts and minds. Southwest Airlines is also one of our favorite examples of High AR for other qualities, specifically because they are Action-Oriented and Resourceful. They were the first airline back in the air after 9/11 and remained profitable during that entire period when others spiraled into bankruptcy.

Another nice example comes from a less widely known company, Broadridge Financial Solutions, Inc., in Lake Success, New York. Broadridge is, however, well known within the financial brokerage services industry, where it has been ranked the number one outsourcing provider, named to the "Best Company to Work For" lists in New York and Canada, and to Gallup's "Best Places to Work Globally," in addition to receiving other awards. John Hogan, Broadridge's president and COO, is acutely aware of the importance of articulating and living purposefully. Speaking at a conference in October 2011 that one of us attended, Hogan talked at length about the power of purpose in terms of how it defines who they want to be as an organization, how they can work together to achieve that ideal, and what they want to individually and collectively leave behind as a legacy.

Like many successful leaders who use word pictures to communicate complex ideas, Hogan tells the story about two stonecutters surrounded by a pile of stones at the edge of a large structure under construction. When asked what they are doing, one replies, "I'm cutting stones." The other one replies, "I'm building a cathedral." Hogan said in a recent presentation that his task and that in his leadership team is to "make the cathedral real." This is done by communicating vividly and continuously about purpose and—here's the good part—"allowing" people to be successful. His task is to find as many ways as possible, consistent with the company's purpose, of enabling people in ways that create value for themselves, their customers, and the organization.

The Psychological Origins of Purpose

Where does a strong sense of purpose come from? Much of the literature regarding purpose and identity has been anecdotal or based on individual and small-group clinical studies. Research on purpose has moved over the past four decades from moral philosophy to clinical psychology to the current interdisciplinary mix of hard and behavioral sciences that measure brain activity, brain chemistry, and genetic sequencing.

Some clinical psychologists and therapists argue that one's purpose may be derived from life experiences that form an individual's narrative or life story. That narrative or story becomes their personal identity and guides subsequent life choices. Bill George and Peter Sims, coauthors of *True North: Discover Your Authentic Leadership*, adopted that perspective in recounting how Howard Schultz, CEO of the world's most well-known coffee company, experienced as a child his father's illness, endured without employer-provided benefits. Schultz vowed that one day a business he created would do more for employees; Starbucks continues to do that admirably well (George & Sims, 2007).

A sense of purpose can also be culturally derived, perhaps strongly influenced by religious doctrine and practice. Rick

Warren's popular book *The Purpose-Driven Life: What on Earth Am I Here For?* has defined life purpose for tens of thousands of Christians, and even influenced political discourse in the 2008 U.S. presidential election (Warren, 2002). Islamic, Jewish, and Eastern thought and practice continue to shape the thinking of billions of followers. Such literature relies on the power of argument, moral imperatives, cultural traditions, and faith, not hard, science-driven research.

Martin E. P. Seligman of the University of Pennsylvania is often credited with launching the positive psychology movement that began blending rigorous clinical and large-group empirical research (Seligman, 2011). Other "positive" research has centered on how individuals create meaning by forming a model of an "ideal self" that becomes "the core mechanism for self-regulation and intrinsic motivation. It is manifest as a personal vision, or an image of what kind of person one wishes to be, what the person hopes to accomplish in life and work" (Boyatzis & Akrivou, 2006, p. 5). Authors such as Kim Cameron, Jane Dutton, and Robert Quinn (2003) have worked diligently at extending the unit of analysis from just the individual to the larger organization and community; their focus has been on three central concerns: positive emotions, positive individual traits, and positive institutions.

The neuroscientists and biogeneticists have now added their voices. Patricia Churchland, a four-decade-long proponent of evolutionary biology, has made the case for basing our sense of morality and ethics on human brain development and its biochemistry, which fuels our cognitive and emotional responses (Churchland, 2011). Others researchers, notably David Rock (2010), have taken the dive into brain biomechanics. They note how a soup of neurochemicals such as oxytocin, corticotrophin (CRH), adrenocorticotropin (ACTH), cortisol, dehydroepiandrosterone (DHEA), dopamine, serotonin, and neuropeptide Y are triggered as our brains process perceived events around us as totally primal flight-fight, threat-reward responses (Serrat, 2010;

Stix, 2011). Those responses are directly linked to human responses that affect individual, team, and organization performance. For Rock, this has led to the creation of "the neuroscience of leadership" (see www.neuroleadership.org) where leaders and coaches can learn to thoughtfully manage how they communicate and act to evoke the "right" positive responses that support greater performance.

Where this research takes leadership, motivation theory, and HR practices is very much up in the air. At its core is a basic stimulus-response (SR) model of human behavior that is grounded in cognitive psychology. This is not how most people think about purpose, which is something more profound and based not in the brain but in the heart—or the soul.

The Toll of Turbulence on Purpose

Although neuroscience applications are fresh and essentially untested, they are helpful for several reasons. Turbulence erodes purpose and identity, and in extreme instances can destroy them. Neuroscience research helps establish the case that brain chemicals have an impact on an individual's sense of purpose and identity when triggered in a response to primal "good-bad" judgments about what is being experienced. As Rock notes (2009): "The threat response is both mentally taxing and deadly to the productivity of a person—or an organization. Because this response uses up oxygen and glucose from the blood, they are diverted from other parts of the brain, including the working memory function, which processes new information and ideas. This impairs analytic thinking, creative insight, and problem solving; in other words, just when people most need their sophisticated mental capabilities, the brain's internal resources are taken away from them" (Rock, 2009, p. 3).

Prolonged rapid and disruptive change causes anxiety and stress and is processed by the brain as flight and threat stimuli, sending cascades of damaging chemicals such as cortisol through our bodies, unless counteracted. If you have to flee a collapsing building, those near-instantaneous responses are lifesaving. Prolonged over weeks, months, or even years without adequate time for recovery, the effects are not just damaging to performance but also to purpose and identity, and can be life-threatening (Dean & Webb, 2011; Hartung & Nagireddy, 2010).

The social consequences are equally profound. Anxiety leads to depression and defensive responses such as disengagement, dissociation (that is, creation of mental defensive boundaries), denial (often expressed as fantasies and myths about others), and physical withdrawal (that is, quitting) (Menzies-Lyth, 1990). When played out in a group or social network, it can lead to "cocooning" where people surround themselves with like-minded people, thus damaging creativity and innovation. For example, Richard Eckersley (2008) contends that religious or secular fundamentalism is all about seeking rigid certainty and control in a world where neither is present. Jonathan Kay, in his 2011 book *Among the Truthers: A Journey Through America's Growing Conspiracist Underground*, remarks how delusional thinking is now being facilitated by Facebook, YouTube, and other social media technologies, intensifying the speed and distance of such thinking.

From a system-dynamics perspective, such responses can lead to positive reinforcing loops that are maladaptive and degenerative. They spread to other team members, and when present in a top management team, can seriously derail an organization. In her 2003 article "Leadership and the Psychology of Turnarounds," Rosabeth Moss Kanter describes a "cycle of decline" that builds momentum as secrecy and denial leads to blame and scorn, avoidance and turf protection, and passivity and helplessness (Kanter, 2003). Similarly, Chris Argyris (1986, 1994) has studied defensive routines in organizations extensively. These routines are made up of undiscussable topics that function to save important people from embarrassment and threat. Inside observers of Enron's death spiral would point to the top team's continued denial of what was in fact occurring, that is, failures to "make the markets" that the company's business model was built on (Madsen & Vance, 2009).

In a recent conversation with Stephen Covey, he pointed out that there is much support for the idea that some stress induced by turbulence evokes higher levels of performance—the concept of *eustress* or good stress, as Hans Seyle (1974) called it. The intense, high-commitment cultures of Southwest Airlines and Starbucks may be good examples. Yet there is also unequivocal evidence that beyond that individual-specific optimal level, it becomes *distress,* which is damaging and leads to fragility (Hartung & Nagireddy, 2010). We believe that the same process occurs at team and organizational levels. A team or organizational culture that fosters a relentless push for performance along with an expectation of unwavering loyalty in a pressure-cooker environment can be a recipe for cynicism and burnout. It is a curvilinear relationship that looks remarkably like the one in Figure 2.2, which contrasts the benefits of greater openness to the environment against its costs.

At a broad level the impact of turbulence and distress are all around us, whether in post-earthquake Japan, Egypt during the Arab Spring, or even the United States, as negative economic and political events mount, institutional responses falter, and social discourse frays. John Casti, author of *Mood Matters: From Rising Skirt Lengths to the Collapse of the World,* notes that the prevailing mood or sentiment of a people about themselves, each other, and their shared future can shape critical choices and actions (Casti, 2010). Moods shaped by turbulent, stressful conditions can have historic consequences.

Making the Case for Wellness

A strong sense of purpose and positive identity are necessary but not sufficient for building and sustaining AR. No matter how vivid, a vision without the ability to realize it promotes only fantasy, not reality. We believe that ability is best secured through physical, psychological, and social wellness. Like agility and resiliency, purpose and wellness are inseparable and together form our capability called Being Purposeful.

The concept of wellness is often misunderstood and misrepresented in the media. It has been taken over by competitive sports, pharmaceutical, sports clothing, and energy-drink companies. Starbucks, for example, announced in November 2011 that it was entering the larger "health and wellness space" with its acquisition of juice company Evolution Fresh Inc., with additional products to come (Jargon, 2011).

Yet wellness is much more than a Gold's Gym fitness program, or a topic discussed while sipping organic juice at a desert yoga retreat. Mind you, we like desert yoga retreats, too, but wellness is increasingly being integrated in the strategies of many companies with sophisticated policies, programs, and practices (Robison, 2010). In a recent *Harvard Business Review* article, "What's the Hard Return on Employee Wellness Programs?," the authors make a solid case for corporate wellness initiatives for economic reasons (Berry, Mirabito, & Baun, 2010). Johnson & Johnson reported $250 million savings in health care costs over only one decade and estimated an ROI of $2.71 for every $1 spent; other companies report as much as a $6 return for every $1 spent. It is becoming clear that healthy employees cost you less.

While health care costs are driving many organizations to create wellness programs, there are other motivators. The annual survey conducted by Towers Watson and the National Business Group on Health demonstrates the linkage between wellness programs and worker performance through such outcomes as lower voluntary attrition and increased work engagement (Towers Watson, 2011). The Gallup organization, in collaboration with Healthways, a wellness program company, publishes a monthly "Well-Being Index" (WBI), a composite index based on surveys of a thousand individuals on 55 different indicators within separate Work Environment, Life Evaluation, Emotional Health, Physical Health, and Healthy Behaviors indices (Gallup-Healthways, 2009). Such data is invaluable for gauging trends and conditions with more than economic impact.

Wellness in Executive Development

We became interested in wellness from designing an executive wellness program as part of a leadership development program for Tampa-based TECO Energy's top sixty executives, and designing a wellness module for an Executive MBA program in collaboration with Mayo Clinic in Jacksonville, Florida. TECO Energy's leadership development program provided the testbed for a holistic leadership approach. The model driving the program attempted to integrate cutting-edge leadership theory and practice with wellness research and practices.

Clint Childress, TECO's senior vice president for corporate services and its chief human resource officer, said in a recent conversation: "The past eight years have been challenging for our company as we've worked to transform it, and we needed our top people to be as resilient as possible. People have been able to take care of themselves and each other to get through this period. It all starts with wellness. Successful change relies on individuals and our organization must be supportive of their development. We're still seeing the fruits of those initiatives in that program."

The Mayo Clinic collaboration around graduate business programs began after watching students arriving for an evening class or beginning two long days of intensive coursework. Many arrived tired, stressed, and often hungry because they were consistently running late. We didn't help much either—the candy bowl in the graduate program office was never empty, the vending machines were filled with junk food, and the coffee shop in the lobby was inaccessible at nights and on weekends. For a program that stressed executive leadership development and care for customers, we had to say enough was enough.

It was time to apply the lessons from the TECO Energy program, this time with Mayo Clinic, which had helped pioneer the executive health program concept in the United States. Open seminars by Mayo staff on stress management, fitness, nutrition, and brain performance were provided to all students. The EMBAs had executive health assessments provided at Mayo Clinic in Jacksonville. The candy bowls went away, lunches and snacks were cleaned up, and even some faculty and staff began losing weight along with the students. Attitudes changed and the size of the seminars began increasing, but this was a voluntary program and didn't reach everyone who needed it. There remains room for improvement.

One of the amazing things learned from this effort was how few other executive education programs in the country were linking wellness and performance. Presentations about the collaboration with Mayo Clinic were made in 2010 at an Executive MBA Council conference. When asked whether their own programs had incorporated wellness initiatives, only three or four hands went up in a room with more than eighty program leaders attending.

Our own experiences added to this clinical practice. This included watching M&A teams perform poorly due to team members' bad diets and physical fitness, coupled with grinding, high-stress workweeks. One of us observed a multibillion-dollar acquisition between two publicly traded companies stumble during negotiations when a key acquiring team member suffered a heart attack. Other teams in other deals would get through the closing stage only to have team members mentally and physically collapse from sheer exhaustion—just when the hard transition and integration work was supposed to start (McCann & Gilkey, 1988).

Three Forms of Wellness

This quick tour of wellness reveals that it is a multidimensional concept. There are many models in use, but all of them have value in focusing attention on important aspects of wellness. We found one model with ten sub-dimensions (www.definitionofwellness .com). Robert Rosen at Healthy Companies International (www .healthycompanies.com) uses a model based on six forms of "healthy leadership." The Mayo Clinic website provides several useful references about the underlying dimensions of this concept (www.mayoclinic.com/health-information/).

Wellness is definitely not limited to individuals and can easily be applied to teams and organizations. At the core, it is individual wellness that is most critical, for reasons discussed shortly. We think the three most important forms of wellness for agility and resiliency in an organizational context are physical, psychological, and social.

Physical Wellness. Physical wellness is defined in terms of nutritional and physical fitness that allows an individual to perform at sustained high levels for long periods. The nutritional and physical aspects are integrally linked. For example, obesity is a national problem in the United States and other nations. Several of the top ten diseases for both men and women in the United States can be linked to poor diet and physical fitness. In the case of heart disease, women are rapidly catching up with men as their work and life pressures mount and their diets and fitness suffer. Dr. Steven Masley designed and delivered the TECO Energy executive fitness program and once directed the Pritikin Longevity Center in Florida. In his book *Ten Years Younger,* he describes premature aging as having almost epidemic scale (Masley, 2005). He contends that poor nutritional and physical fitness are the main culprits.

Nutritionists and biomedical researchers understand a lot about how food composition affects our state of mind and our physical performance, but much is still unknown. Educating ourselves about health and wellness is the starting point. Josiah Pritchard in Mayo Clinic's Executive Health Program in Jacksonville has identified several key Web resources, and we offer them in Exhibit 4.1.

Exhibit 4.1. Mayo Clinic's Josiah Pritchard's Favorite Wellness Web Resources

Health—Physical and Psychological

1. Mayo Clinic's open-access websites:
    http://www.mayoclinic.com
    http://www.mayoclinic.com/health
        /HealthyLivingIndex/HealthyLivingIndex
2. Centers for Disease Control and Prevention
    http://www.cdc.gov
3. National Institutes of Health
    http://www.nih.gov
4. American Diabetes Association
    http://www.diabetes.org
5. Blue Zones
    http://Bluezones.com
6. American Heart Association
    http://www.heart.org/HEARTORG/
7. Healthways corporate wellness organization website:
    http://www.healthways.com/about/default
    .aspx?id=75
8. *USA Today* wellness website:
    http://yourlife.usatoday.com/health

9. *NY Times Magazine* wellness website:
   http://www.nytimes.com/pages/health
   /index.html
10. SparkPeople.com—An online diet and healthy living community:
    http://www.sparkpeople.com
11. Creativity for Life!—An online resource for promoting creative thinking and action:
    http://creativityforlife.com
12. active.com—A central online resource for active people and events:
    http://www.active.com
13. Livestrong.com—The outdoor exercise partner website with Lance Armstrong's LIVESTRONG Foundation:
    http://www.livestrong.com
14. The President's Council on Fitness, Sports and Nutrition (PCFSN) online resource:
    http://fitness.gov
15. fitness.com—An online community dedicated to all things related to wellness:
    http://fitness.com
16. MapMyRUN—An online community dedicated to all things related to running:
    http://mapmyrun.com
17. Lose It!—An online resource for healthy dieting:
    http://www.loseit.com

Community Engagement

1. Corporation for National and Community Service:
   http://Serve.gov
2. American Red Cross:
   http://www.redcross.org/en/volunteer

Nutritional wellness requires knowledge and discipline about food intake—quantity, kind, and combinations—that supports sustained mind and body performance. This means not only managing one's own nutrition but also supporting others in doing so. We're not talking about the fanaticism of a strict vegan software development team in Cupertino, but a willingness to share with one's coworkers and associates that healthier alternatives are possible.

Physical wellness goes hand in hand with nutritional wellness and remains a passionate subject for many who have it, seek it, and deny it. Claims and counterclaims abound about different forms of physical activity, different ways of participating, and how much. It is now clear that companies—perhaps especially those that rely on the performance of sedentary knowledge workers—need to pay attention to the physical well-being of their employees. The links between brain functioning and cardiovascular health are well established. Stress is a killer, and learning how to self-manage our responses to it is a big step. Learning to use exercise and fitness to boost stamina and brain functioning are other steps. It also means knowing when and how to access medical support services, including doctors and trainers, to assist you. Physical wellness also requires knowledge and discipline about engaging in physical activities that promote high performance and minimize the damaging effects of physical and mental stress.

Josiah Pritchard at Mayo Clinic also directed us to Dan Buettner's book *Thrive: Finding Happiness the Blue Zones Way* (2010). Buettner examines wellness patterns and wellness disciplines around the world and offers four general guidelines, each of which he elaborates: move naturally, develop the right outlook, eat wisely, and cultivate connections with others. The nations where the patterns of practices associated with each of these rules are among the highest include Denmark, Singapore and, perhaps surprisingly, Mexico. They are what Buettner calls the "Blue Zones" where people are thriving and happiness is generally higher. Wellness can be a national (ecosystem-level) development target.

Psychological Wellness. Psychological wellness has two aspects, cognitive wellness and emotional wellness. A cognitively well individual can efficiently perceive, process, and retrieve large amounts of diverse and novel information, even in periods of stress. Higher-level brain functioning is essential for quick and accurate sensemaking, which gives meaning to this information. Chapter Five on Being Aware deals with this aspect of cognitive wellness.

The direct link to nutritional and physical fitness is clear, as certain vitamins, minerals, and nutriments, along with a healthy cardiovascular system, promote high brain performance. However, highly turbulent environments damage brain performance and sensemaking due to excessive physical and mental stress. Stimulating and developing brain performance to build systems thinking, creativity, and complex problem solving should be a goal for everyone.

Emotional wellness means that you have a keen awareness and mastery of your emotions, which contributes to a positive but realistic self-concept. For a manager it also means recognizing when an individual is distressed and his or her emotions begin playing a defining role in work performance. It is OK, indeed healthy, for you to express emotions at work and to help others deal with situations that evoke their emotions. It is not OK to let unchecked emotions dictate how you respond to challenging conditions. Cognitive wellness means being responsible for your emotions and behaviors.

The links to the other forms of wellness are obvious. When you are feeling strong and healthy, your brain is likely to be functioning effectively in assessing and making sense of a situation. Fight-flight and threat-reward interpretations will tend to produce a different emotional response than when you feel overwhelmed, exhausted, or ravenous—and inclined to wolf down the bad stuff that's all around today's offices or grab a quick energy drink. Neuroscience advocates like Rock have not fully factored these additional wellness elements into their models of mind/body performance.

Social Wellness. We are social animals and do not do well for long without social contact and relationships. We learn from others, share feelings and ideas with others, and express empathy for others. Whether Victor Frankl in a Nazi concentration camp; Tom Hanks in the film *Cast Away*, stranded alone on a tropical island in the South Pacific; or just about any one of us, it seems to be critical to engage with others to share feelings, test reality, and meet shared needs.

A socially well individual develops and sustains satisfying relationships in a family or living arrangement, at work within a team or group, in the community through voluntary associations, and even in the larger world through donations to charitable causes, political advocacy, or direct voluntary action to improve the shared human experience (R. D. Putnam, 2000). This need to connect at the level of shared human experience takes many people toward some form of spiritual inquiry and religious faith. Perhaps this is why evidence shows that being engaged in a faith-based community promotes positive mood, self-esteem, and longevity (Buettner, 2010).

Researchers have shown that individuals lacking social wellness in terms of relationships experience greater illness, have death rates two to three times higher than those having good relationships, and do less well under stress. Going it alone during long periods of high stress due to rapid change and disruption is disastrous for AR.

Preconditions for Purposefulness

We now have the basis for a model that relates purpose and wellness with AR and turbulence in the environment. In Figure 4.1

Figure 4.1. Relationships Between Purpose, Wellness, and Turbulence

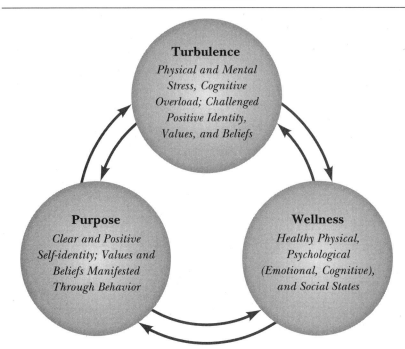

we suggest a negative relationship between the prevailing level of turbulence experienced and wellness; turbulence has a negative impact on physical, psychological, and social wellness, but attention to wellness builds physical and psychological stamina, which ameliorates the negative impact of turbulence. There is also the strong, positive relationship between wellness and purpose; attention to the three forms of wellness supports a positive self-identity, values, and beliefs. Conversely, a poor sense of self-identity and unsupportive values and beliefs can undermine wellness.

As one of our five capabilities, Being Purposeful by itself does not assure sufficient High AR. Purposefulness does provide the foundation needed, and if it is compromised, then it could be a serious, potentially fatal flaw in building agility and resiliency.

It fully contributes when three preconditions are met: Clarity, "Right" Fit, and Alignment.

The Need for Clarity

First, there has to be clarity and tangible expression of the values and beliefs underlying purposefulness at each level in our model. Peter Senge notes how a lack of clarity is one of the reasons why visions do not take hold in an organization (Senge, 1990). Lack of clarity results in fuzzy values and beliefs that leave room for too many interpretations and potential conflicts. Fuzziness gets organizations into trouble. There are too many opportunities for individuals and groups to *not* buy into the vision and to act independently; this is what is called the "agency problem" in economics. Think of the derivatives traders at Lehman, Merrill, or Goldman Sachs where the sheer amounts of money to be made constantly threatened to overwhelm standards of professional conduct.

The Need for "Right" Fit

Second, the values and beliefs underlying organization purpose must be appropriate—that is, they must be "right" in that they fit the conditions encountered. For example, values of self-reliance that reward go-it-alone action when collaborative action is required undermine AR, and Richard Sennett (2005) claims that poor fit between an organization's demands and employee moral compasses "corrodes character." What are "right" values and beliefs? We believe that three of them transcend all situations and levels:

- *Continuous learning.* The organization must encourage and support continuous learning at all levels.
- *Sustainable shared progress.* The organization must view itself as part of society and an integral means of creating and sharing value (Porter & Kramer, 2011).

- *Distinctive contribution.* We all want to make a distinctive contribution and be part of something exceptional. The belief in empowerment and self-efficacy must be a prerequisite for individual and team purpose (Covey, 2004).

The Need for Alignment

Finally, there must be alignment or consistency of purpose across levels such that they fully reinforce and support each other. Alignment of purpose across levels is a critical design feature for High AR that we will discuss further in Chapter Six. Senge, Collins and Porras, and Covey would all acknowledge that requirement, but turbulence challenges all four levels in varying ways and intensity. Turbulence is unevenly experienced within an organization, making alignment across levels one of the major AR management challenges.

Other observers have noted the toxic consequences of this growing misalignment (Frost, 2007). Robert Goldfarb, writing in the *New York Times,* noted: "Call it trickle-down anxiety. Accustomed to hearing about budget cuts and layoffs from on high, employees at every level are becoming risk-adverse. Dedicated, ambitious workers tell me they are so afraid of making a mistake that they feel it's safer for their careers to avoid innovation and initiative. Managers need to realize that this paralysis threatens their companies' health" (Goldfarb, 2011, p. 8). He goes on to note how experienced management teams are beginning to fracture, as well, and the cumulative effect is like "drawing the oxygen from the workplace" (Goldfarb, 2001, p. 8).

Misalignment between the individual, team, and organization is visible everywhere. At a time when senior executive compensation is at an all-time high, the rest of the troops are suffering financially. The reward and employee engagement gap between top management and the middle and lower levels is widening in most organizations. No wonder, then, that Aon Hewitt found in its 2011 *Talent Survey* report that employee engagement levels were at all-time lows (Aon Hewitt, 2011). Of course, in his 2001 book *Free Agent Nation,* Daniel Pink had already tapped that sentiment when he noted, "Beneath the radar of the political and media establishment, tens of millions of Americans have become free agents" (Pink, 2001, p. 11). Larry Hirschhorn also notes, in *Reworking Authority* (1997): "Today it seems that companies have never been more careless about the people they employ: layoffs, closings and consolidations have put an end to presumed careers and long-held jobs throughout the economy" (Hirschhorn, 1997, p. 118). Hirschhorn points out that this kind of behavior fosters resentments, grievances, distrust, cynicism, and undermines the "culture of openness" needed to operate well in a turbulent environment. Serious indicators of misalignment, indeed.

Building High AR Across Levels

Consistent with our theme, Being Purposeful has maximum impact when expressed at multiple levels—the individual, team, organization, and larger ecosystem levels.

Individuals Being Purposeful

Much of this chapter has taken an individual perspective, so here we only want to drive home two key guidelines. First, develop the mindset and practical skills for listening to yourself, reflecting on what is experienced, felt, and done in response. For a well and responsible manager this means attending workshops, seminars, and actively reading to acquire those skills to clarify what one believes and why. A personal vision statement should be created that truly means something and serves as a guide. Post it in the office and at home and refer to it for guidance when conditions become truly challenging. This statement should include clear declarations about what you personally value and believe, how you will contribute to the benefit of others, and what you expect in return. Act on it and help others in *their* process of self-mastery.

Second, make the commitment during self-reflection to improve what you discover and don't like. Seek help if the path to improvement seems overwhelming and involves acquiring lots of new knowledge and skills. Most important, take responsibility for your own wellness. This may indeed feel overwhelming for anyone who has compromised his or her wellness and now wants to correct it. From our experience nothing reinforces purpose and identity more than regaining your health. Your performance at work and your satisfaction with life will prove it.

It is part of your responsibility to demand wellness at work. We are amazed by both how much and how little progress has been made in cleaning up work environments to support wellness in all its forms. Request action and then be more emphatic, if necessary, about eliminating or at least reducing the things getting in the way of greater wellness. That may mean eliminating the massive amounts of junk food around the office and replacing it with better alternatives. We had occasion to have lunch in the Microsoft Campus Commons building one day at the company's Redmond, Washington, headquarters. We watched hundreds of employees, mostly Millennials, choose between a dozen different cuisines at different serving locations, all pretty well balanced and nutritious. The Commons offered a well-populated volleyball court out back, a gym nearby, and a busy sports gear shop along one hallway. More and more companies are accommodating personal wellness choices, and they know it makes a difference in recruiting and retaining talent.

It could also mean reducing excessive and unproductive work. Intense working periods need to be counterbalanced by opportunities for free time, exercise, and stress management. We know one company with such a macho culture that no one wanted to be the first out of the parking lot at night; instead, the goal was to be the last one to leave. Was work getting done? No, some people played computer games until others gave up and left. This was silly and damaging to work performance and social wellness. Correcting such dysfunctional practices is easier when people speak up.

Teams Being Purposeful

For a team or group, the added dynamic is the interplay of multiple value/belief systems that shape group behavior. This dynamic is the stuff of legends in management, whether the new product innovation team in Tracy Kidder's *Soul of a New Machine* (1981), or the group of senior leaders and administrators staving off global financial collapse in Andrew Ross Sorkin's *Too Big to Fail* (2009). Academics tell us that goal congruence within a top management team can be linked to organization performance, but how such congruence can be achieved is a challenge (Colbert, Kristof-Brown, Bradley, & Barrick, 2008). From a purposefulness perspective, there are two basic guidelines.

First, self-mastery practiced individually means considering how your thoughts and actions impact others on the team. This is a holistic inquiry that means examining the complex interplay of your own values and beliefs and wellness dimensions, particularly emotional wellness, with other team members. This is the basis for effective work in teams. Ideally, such reflection should be under both normal and extreme conditions to understand how differences may appear. Doing this well may require the help of a mentor, coach, or therapist. In addition, there are many validated instruments to assist; we suggest finding one that allows self-reflection under extreme conditions, such as the Hogan Development Survey that identifies "derailer" characteristics under pressure, assessment tools offered by the Center for Creative Leadership or by A&DC, a U.K.-based consultancy.

Second, it's about the team and there is a need to accept responsibility for each other. The performance of any team is a function of the skills and capabilities of its members, plus the unique dynamics and synergy generated among the members. Forging an effective group process and avoiding negative synergy may be supported by HR professionals. We recall CEOs like the late John Robson, a *compadre* of Donald Rumsfeld from their Searle days together, whose eyes would light up when talking about taking leadership teams through Outward Bound. Our point is that it is important to really understand how each individual and the team collectively operates under varying conditions.

The goal for any such team-based exercises is to surface and work on the operative values, beliefs, and wellness issues present in a team *before* the team faces a situation of extreme stress and pressure. This requires emotional intelligence at the level of the team and candor among its members that may be difficult to achieve.

Organizations Being Purposeful

Dozens of insightful authors have already said a great deal about the importance of organization purpose, expressed as a compelling and widely embraced vision. To this we also added the organization's role in promoting wellness to support that vision. We believe that the organization level is where most development for promoting purpose and wellness is likely to occur, so it is worth reiterating some guidelines here.

Statements of purpose can be undervalued and too easily trivialized by many organization leaders. They tend to be mundane, vanilla-flavored statements that provide the barest and most basic standards, or exhortations of fanciful dreams that employees find implausible at best. Contrast that with the Southwest Airlines example cited earlier. Colleen Barrett, the former executive secretary who became Herb Kelleher's hand-picked choice for president of Southwest, said that when they were starting up the company, the goal was to "democratize the skies" (Blanchard & Barrett, 2010, p. 68), which meant make flying affordable for both business and pleasure. In *Nuts!* Kevin and Jackie Freiberg detail sixteen "Business Basics" or core values that drive Southwest (Freiberg & Freiberg, 1996). Those values haven't changed much since then and, to a person, Southwest employees we have talked with get it, which is why they work where they do.

The challenge is clearly to ensure that purpose as vision is shared well beyond the organization's top leadership team. The powerful brands—Starbucks, Patagonia, Toyota, Apple—know this well. What they tap through their own unique identity enables others to articulate and realize their own *individual* and *team* purpose and identity. This experience is much bigger than simply embracing an organization's strategy, which does not occur if the strategy is not aligned with the organization's vision and purpose.

Betrayal of the responsibility for defining purpose by not behaving in ways consistent with the organization's purpose can be treated harshly, as Enron, Lehman Brothers, and the "too big to fail" banks like Goldman Sachs can attest. The tragedy today is that betrayals have become so common that the public, as well as specific stakeholders, such as employees, have become numbed to them and quite cynical (Sennett, 2005). When Google violates user trust and their code of "Don't be evil" (http://investor.google.com/corporate/code-of-conduct.html), should we stop using their services? A monetary fine and public *mea culpa* do little to change corporate behaviors or public perceptions. However, the cumulative impact of flagrant and repeated violations may be revealed if the environment becomes hostile and the organization's survival threatened. The Occupy Wall Street protests in late 2011 were only a test case.

Finally, thousands of U.S. companies are discovering that promoting wellness in all its forms produces major economic and performance benefits. We have said a great deal about this, but here we want to emphasize the AR aspects of wellness. Some companies figured out this connection years ago. PricewaterhouseCoopers (PwC) and Deloitte were doing a great job burning out their young talent, long before achieving partner status, with grueling work schedules that damaged young families and worker engagement. Then each firm began supporting work-life balance initiatives, such as mandatory vacation time and reduced travel time away from home, with positive outcomes.

Ecosystems Being Purposeful

At an ecosystem level, the global economic competitiveness of entire industries may depend on the prevailing level of wellness of companies within them. Health care plans for retired auto workers, state government workers, and many other employee groups are major drags on the financial health of some organizations in those sectors. A global supply chain can only be as agile and resilient as its members.

More fundamentally, the historic demographic shift where older, perhaps less agile and resilient (that is, less well) workforces begin to dominate some industries, even national populations, is making global economic competitiveness even more challenging. Japanese companies, for example, have had to move many of their operations out of Japan to get access to younger, better-trained workers as Japan's population ages. This is also increasingly true in Europe and the United States.

For an organization, working "up and out" means making sure that its purpose is manifested and supported even at a global level. For example, in the 1990s Nike ran afoul of labor activist groups because of the poor work conditions in many of its supplier plants in Southeast Asia. Nike worked to improve those conditions and established an audit program for its supplier factories. More recently, Apple found itself confronting similar poor work conditions in a Chinese iPhone supplier plant where there had been at least seventeen worker suicides and multiple worker protests (Johnson, 2011). Apple put pressure on its supplier, Foxconn, to improve conditions with uncertain results.

In our interdependent world, no firm can operate autonomously from its suppliers, customers, nongovernmental advocacy groups, and other stakeholders. Accepting your organization's role in larger society should be assumed and incorporated in a dynamic and flexible program of corporate social responsibility. If you believe in the value of a healthy natural environment, then you have the responsibility to bring others along with you. Companies like Walmart have come to embrace this idea with their initiative starting in 2009 regarding environmental standards for its thousands of vendors. We take a closer look at how they did this in Chapter Nine.

Don Buettner, in his 2010 book *Blue Zones* (cited earlier), also talks about the importance of carefully selecting your "tribe." By this he means that an individual should pick friends thoughtfully and join those who support and reinforce values and beliefs, particularly regarding wellness. This also applies at the ecosystem level. Apple took a hit to its reputation—its legitimacy of purpose— by contracting with a Chinese supplier that engaged in shoddy workplace practices. Organizations should team with other firms that inspire them to do better. That is why networks of organizations such as those established by the United Nations Global Compact (UNGC), World Business Council for Sustainable Development, or Aspen Institute are so valuable.

The U.S. military learned a lesson from the wars in Iraq and Afghanistan: that taking care of a soldier's family at home has a direct impact on that soldier's performance on the front line. Businesses have an equivalent responsibility of ensuring that local institutions such as educational systems, social-welfare nonprofits, and civil society organizations are healthy—that is, supported by volunteers and monetary resources sufficient to help the community thrive and support people in times of need. Weak community support systems undermine workforce families and workers. Relatedly, Richard Florida has made a compelling case that organizations directly benefit from locating in communities that are attractive to the creative professionals needed for them to grow in a global economy (Florida, 2005, 2010).

Finally, when bad behavior or unacceptable work practices by another organization damages the credibility and legitimacy of all others, there is an obligation to speak out early about it. Ecosystems, like organizations, need to manage themselves and how they are perceived. Professional associations and groups become essential in this process, and groups like the National Association of Corporate Directors (NACD) have played an important role in improving corporate governance expectations and professional standards. In general, however, industries are not good at self-policing, and the government may need to step into the breach. The Sarbanes-Oxley 2002 accounting regulations and the 2010 Dodd-Frank financial-services regulations arguably demonstrate what can happen when an industry doesn't do a good job.

Summary

This rather lengthy chapter has ranged from a discussion of neurochemicals to global supply chains. Binding these topics has been the common theme of creating and sustaining purposefulness. We began by stressing the foundational role of purpose and wellness in supporting High AR and tried to demonstrate how they are manifested. While our words convey information that ideally provides perspective and direction for further inquiry, what we know from our research and listening to company executives and line managers is that clarity and alignment of the right values and beliefs, supported by practices and conditions that support wellness in all three forms, creates and sustains a powerful sense of purposefulness. When environments speed up and shocks arrive all too frequently, Being Purposeful provides the foundation for moving confidently to create opportunity and survive setbacks.

chapter
FIVE

Building and
Sustaining Awareness

As early as 2005, NYU professor Nouriel Roubini, along with a few other nay-saying Cassandras, had been speaking to anyone who would listen about what he saw as a great looming financial disaster precipitated by housing speculation and credit. Few listened until it happened, and Roubini moved from Cassandra to Oracle status (Mihm, 2008). Despite reports from various intelligence groups that Islamic terrorists were filtering into the United States and that attacks using commercial aircraft were possible, 9/11 happened anyway (Eldridge, Ginsburg, Hempel, Kephart, & Moore, 2004; Watkins & Bazerman, 2003). In both instances, information was present for organization decision makers that was not acted on. Why? Thousands of pages have been written about how these events occurred, but at the core is what we call Being Aware.

This chapter is about how you know what you know. How you sense, interpret, and act based on information outside as well as inside the organization is critically important as the two preceding examples illustrate. At this very moment, can you name the five or six most significant emerging trends within your organization's environment that are vital to its future performance, perhaps even its existence? How much agreement is there about these trends within your top leadership team? Across other management levels and businesses? What are you and the teams in the organization doing with that knowledge to craft effective responses? How quickly? These are vital questions about mindfulness—an awareness of self in context—and all deserving good answers.

Being Aware surfaced as one of the most important features of High AR in our research. Like our Being Purposeful capability, awareness is manifested through appropriate skills, tools, and practices at each of the four levels. In Chapter Four we noted how core values and beliefs and the level of cognitive wellness determine how effectively we respond. An organization's action orientation, discussed in Chapter Six, also depends on the quality of those awareness skills, tools, and practices. In his 2009 book *The New Know: Innovation Powered by Analytics*, Thornton May makes an eloquent case that how we once learned and "know what we know" has dramatically begun changing in response to information overload. For May, the use of higher-powered analytic tools, processes, practices, and specialized analytic roles is the best way to deal with this challenge.

We think that such tools are extremely useful, but a more comprehensive, strategic perspective is called for. Our involvement with the three Oxford Futures Forums held to date at Oxford University's Saïd Business School has demonstrated the power of conceptual tools such as scenarios in making sense of organizational environments (Ramirez, Selsky, & van der Heijden, 2010). Strategic focus comes not only from stepping in close with the right analytic tools, but also from stepping back and taking an expansive view.

So, How Do You Know What You Know?

The answer to this question begins with sensemaking—how you construct a reality of what you are experiencing. This is not a philosophical abstraction, as a case in point illustrates. In the late 1980s Joe Porac and colleagues (2011) studied the Scottish knitwear industry. This prospering industry was composed of a small group of firms, many family-owned, that manufactured high-end sweaters. Profitability and market share, however, have declined for more than twenty years because these firms persisted in seeing only each other as their competitors—and not the new players from Italy and China. In their mental model of their industry, those new competitors were inconceivable, and therefore invisible.

We believe that this question is best answered from the perspectives of knowledge management (KM) and organizational learning (OL). Whereas KM is most associated with organizational and ecosystem level learning processes (for example, learning with others in a global supply chain), OL is a concept that spans all four AR levels. Both are integrally concerned with how we recognize and create a coherent view of our world, which is becoming increasingly difficult as turbulence accelerates.

As the amount and variety of information explode, and the ways we create and access it multiply, managers become more prone to information overload. Overload feels threatening and evokes dysfunctional responses like those described in Chapter Four. It also increases the danger of information *under*load—blind spots that cause managers to miss critical information that could make a competitive difference if acted on early enough, or that could help avoid a collision with an unfolding event.

In a *Wired* magazine article adapted from his book *The Shallows: What the Internet Is Doing to Our Brains*, Nicholas Carr (2010) made a stinging indictment that "the riot of information from the Internet shatters our focus and rewires our brain" (Carr, 2010,

p. 112). From a neuropsychological perspective the rewiring is real, and one result is a growing inability to focus attention on important information for sustained periods. Adding to the criticism, Derek Dean and Caroline Webb (2011), writing in *McKinsey Quarterly*, make the case: "For all the benefits of the information and communications revolution, it has a well-known dark side: information overload and its close cousin, attention fragmentation. These scourges hit CEOs and their colleagues in the C-suite particularly hard because senior executives so badly need uninterrupted time to synthesize information from many different sources, reflect on its implications for the organization, apply judgment, make trade-offs, and arrive at good decisions" (Dean & Webb, 2011, p. 3).

Awareness Through KM and OL

The KM perspective provides a way of understanding the overall process of externally acquiring, internally building and sharing, applying, and retaining useful knowledge to respond to knowledge challenges posed by the environment (McCann & Buckner, 2004). A knowledge challenge is the gap between what the organization currently knows and must know in the future. Figure 5.1 illustrates the relationships among these KM subprocesses.

There was a burst of interest in KM in the late 1990s from a variety of authors (Davenport & Prusak, 1998; de Geus, 1997; Edvinsson & Malone, 1997; Nonaka & Takeuchi, 1995; Stewart, 1997), but it is actually Peter Drucker who coined the concepts of "knowledge economy," "knowledge worker," and "knowledge organization" more than two decades earlier (Drucker, 1969, 1973, 1985). There are now several academic journals, such as the *Journal of Knowledge Management*, dedicated to KM practices, and spending on KM-related systems easily runs in the tens of billions

Figure 5.1. A Strategic KM Framework

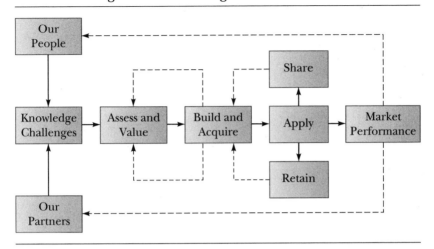

of dollars each year. KM is alive and well, although many operational challenges exist in scaling it up.

There were multiple trends spurring the early interest in KM, such as the increasing amounts and diversity of information and need to efficiently share information across a hundred national borders. What kicked KM into high gear, however, was the realization that unique knowledge, when managed effectively, produces intellectual capital which, in turn, can yield durable competitive advantage.

High AR Aware organizations view their knowledge as intellectual capital and treat it as a competitive asset. KM in many organizations has rightfully become a strategic priority and an actively managed set of integrated processes. Describing the design elements and issues associated with large-scale KM systems is beyond the scope of this book, but we believe that leaders within High AR organizations

- Attend systematically to how their organization learns and adapts, using broadly understood conceptual frameworks that have process owners and managers

- Cultivate a future-focused mindset that frames current and future learning needs in terms of "knowledge challenges"—the gaps between what their organization currently knows and must know in five or ten years
- Integrate KM with the strategic decision-making process to ensure that they have the right knowledge to produce high-quality decisions
- Operationally link knowledge to product/service/process innovation routines to assure the greatest knowledge-added content
- Effectively integrate hard and soft systems, such as IT systems and communities of practice, within accessible knowledge platforms that share the right information at the right place and time

Leaders also deploy practices and processes within HR to promote the use, sharing, and retention of knowledge. For example, they link training and development to the specific identified knowledge gaps and needs. They develop cultures that reward knowledge creation, application, and open sharing. They also work diligently at retaining knowledge creators and mentors (Key, Thompson, & McCann, 2009; McCann & Buckner, 2004). Few organizations we know can lose 20 to 30 percent of their knowledge workers over a ten-year period due to economic recession or demographic shifts without performance problems.

OL—The Foundation for KM

Closely related to KM is the organizational learning (OL) perspective. Management scholars first explored this perspective in the 1970s, and Bo Hedberg's 1980 book chapter "How Organizations Learn and Unlearn" is a classic summary of this early work. Peter Senge's *The Fifth Discipline* (1990) was a breakthrough in linking OL with systems thinking. OL is fundamentally concerned with how you perceive, interpret, and respond to what you experience in your environment. What you have already learned from previous interactions with the environment shapes the ways you respond—predictably or creatively, proactively or reactively, slowly or quickly.

What is an organization that it may learn? Argyris and Schön asked this question as the title of the first chapter of their 1978 book *Organizational Learning: A Theory of Action Perspective*. Clearly, individuals and teams within them learn, but organizations do engage in activities that meet some conditions for learning, for example, archived knowledge being analogous to an individual's memory. Hedberg (1980) concludes that "Organizations, as such, do not learn; members of organizations learn. . . . Although organizational learning occurs through individuals, it would be a mistake to conclude that organizational learning is nothing but the cumulative result of their members' learning. Organizations do not have brains, but they have cognitive systems and memories" (p. 6).

KM and OL perspectives permanently change how you look at and think about the world. Though perhaps not as powerful as Morpheus (Laurence Fishburne) providing Neo (Keanu Reeves) the means to visualize "the Matrix," KM and OL are powerful frame-shifting perspectives. For example, in their 2003 *Harvard Business Review* article "Preparing for Evil," Ian Mitroff and Murat Alpaslan (2003) make the case that companies have to prepare for "abnormal accidents," not just "normal accidents" and "natural accidents." This requires radically new skills and ways of looking at situations: "If they are to cope with abnormal crises, companies must learn to see—as their enemies do—skyscrapers as vertical coffins and aircraft as flying bombs, ugly and horrifying though that prospect may be" (p. 110).

Mitroff and Alpaslan also pose an interesting question as to whether the crises and shocks that seem to be rocking organizations more frequently are the result of learning failures—that is, the results of misreads between reality and filtered perceptions. We concur with Peter Senge that "learning disabilities" in organizations arise from ignorance or misreading of the systemic structure of a situation, and this deficient awareness can lead to all kinds of problems. However, it is necessary to understand our three core principles of OL to appreciate how learning failures occur.

Continuous Active Learning Assumed

First, learning failures happen when you stop learning. Being Aware assumes continuous active learning. This is active learning that requires continuously rethinking and restructuring what you know—"tearing down obsolete mental maps and starting anew" (Hedberg, 1980, p. 4). This is also learning that challenges assumptions and existing ways of doing things. Some have called this "double loop learning"; others have called it "frame breaking," referring to the dialectical "framing and reframing" process in which meaning or perspective is first given for a situation or event then changed (Argyris & Schön, 1978). Viewing a skyscraper as a vertical coffin rather than a work habitat can lead to very different ways of thinking about building design.

There are several learning skills associated with active learning. For example, active learners are known to be open-minded and capable of embracing alternative views. Active learners are also inquisitive and curious by nature about many things, and they can think critically about what they see. These are typically elements found in the leadership competency models created in many organizations.

Southwest Airlines provides an example. Herb Kelleher, Southwest's founder, and Colleen Barrett, its president, are described as "both intensely inquisitive. Barrett is willing to try almost anything once and is responsible for bringing many new ideas into the company. Kelleher is a student of life and a voracious reader who digs deeply into issues to understand them thoroughly" (Freiberg & Freiberg, 1996, p. 113).

That quality is aided by another essential competency, systems thinking—the ability to view things, and yourself, as interconnected elements of more expansive, dynamic systems that are coevolving with you. Systems thinkers accept complexity as an inherent quality of what they see. And within a global economy, two related characteristics are a global mindset and cultural flexibility.

Finally, a skill often given too little attention in a discussion about adaptive learning is the ability to effectively communicate through multiple means about what is learned; you must be able to articulate and share knowledge if it is to be useful. Easier said than done when the perceived trends or events are still early in their evolution, ill-defined, and perhaps even contentious.

Are people who have these characteristics extremely unusual, rare individuals? Not really. We know that these specific characteristics are partially inherent, but they are also developed through life experiences such as a Peace Corps stint. Active learning characteristics can also be measured and assessed using a variety of instruments in a selection process. Individuals and teams can then acquire many of these through specially designed education and training opportunities. The fact is that some people are still simply better at these skills than others, and those are the individuals most needed in critical awareness roles in an organization.

It's About Sensemaking

Second, learning failures happen when sensemaking lapses. An organization engages in sensemaking interactions with its environments (Weick, 1988) based on its members' "cognitive maps" and "theories of action" (Argyris & Schön, 1978). Just as you have a cognitive structure of reality, an organization's cognitive map is a collective construction about its existing internal and external relationships and why they matter. Its theory of action describes how cause-and-effect relationships exist among those things and what will happen to other parts of the map when something changes—what we call action hypotheses. Altering your own cognitive maps and theories of action is potent when it incorporates self-reflection and forces you to ask new questions to meet new circumstances—in other words, you experience unlearning then relearning (Argyris, 1986).

Creating the conditions for learning and unlearning to occur freely and safely within and across individuals, teams, organizations, and ecosystems is the prime task for Being Aware. This does not occur spontaneously; sensemaking can fail when novel events challenge prevailing mental models but people do not realize it, do not have alternative models at the ready, or cannot adapt to the new conditions (Weick & Sutcliffe, 2007). Much resistance to change stems from such sensemaking failures.

Many high-tech companies foster effective sensemaking and improve their awareness through systematic "knowledge bridging," which links seemingly unrelated fields of research or bodies of knowledge to create new products and services (Hsu & Lim, 2006). Companies intentionally create situations and settings to challenge prevailing ideas by bringing together diverse people and knowledge bases. Additional strategies to keep minds open and promote diverse knowledge sharing certainly need the support of leaders.

Turbulence Erodes Awareness

Third, learning failures occur when mental maps, models, and theories of action are overwhelmed by relentless change. If active learning does not occur and essential KM processes are underdeveloped for the prevailing level of turbulence, then opportunities are missed and risk exposures are increased. Prevailing cognitive maps and theories of action serve wonderful uses, but they also have double edges. On the one hand, they can facilitate rapid sensemaking and action because they rely on tried and proven models of the world. On the other hand, using tried and proven ways for looking at totally new conditions can lead to disaster. Executives at Lehman Brothers, for example, used conventional, albeit anemic, investment industry risk management processes to manage global traders who were packaging and selling billions of dollars of complex mortgage-backed derivatives that few understood.

Five Core Awareness Processes

It is often necessary to abandon invalid cognitive maps and models as you would any broken tool and then create more appropriate ones that better meet conditions. We offer up a useful replacement model based on five Awareness processes: Scanning, Sensemaking, Shaping, Sharing, and Storing. These five processes focus attention and get you to ask the right questions about the quality of the Awareness capability in your organization. Figure 5.2 summarizes these five core processes.

Scanning

Searching an environment for information and knowledge is fundamental to cognitive functioning. There are several operational choices and routines associated with scanning that make significant differences in how effectively it occurs. There must be recognition that active, systematic scanning is critical to agility and resiliency, reflected in the sustained investment of time and effort devoted to it. Such scanning must also be premeditated and rigorous. For you personally, this means taking the time to read multiple, diverse sources of information regularly. For a team, it means making the time to share with each other what you are hearing and reading. These aren't just watercooler or

Figure 5.2. Five Core Awareness Processes

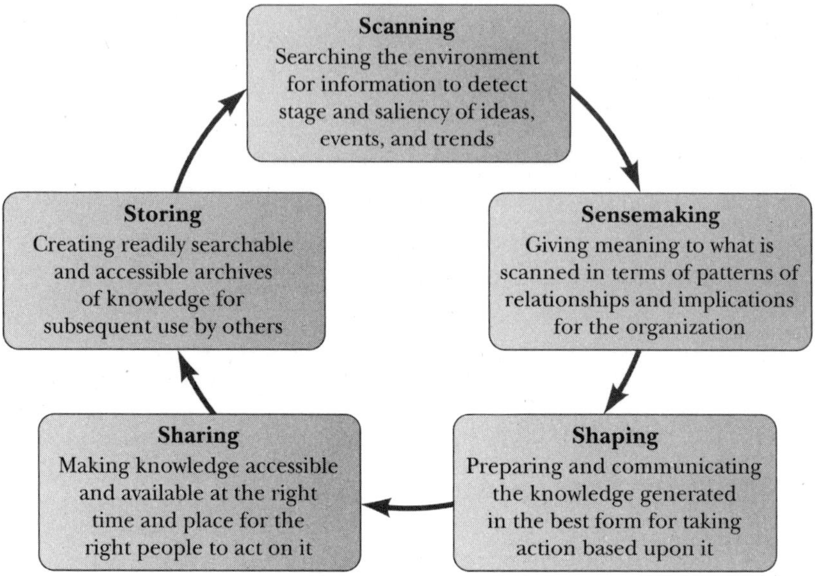

Scanning
Searching the environment for information to detect stage and saliency of ideas, events, and trends

Storing
Creating readily searchable and accessible archives of knowledge for subsequent use by others

Sensemaking
Giving meaning to what is scanned in terms of patterns of relationships and implications for the organization

Sharing
Making knowledge accessible and available at the right time and place for the right people to act on it

Shaping
Preparing and communicating the knowledge generated in the best form for taking action based upon it

hallway chats, but regularly planned encounters to pool and validate information.

For the organization, it may mean investing resources in a specialized internal staff function that searches and assimilates information from multiple sources, or spending money on industry associations and lobbyists. Or it may mean making sure that travel budgets stay intact to allow people to fan out across the globe and return with new knowledge about what is happening. Companies like Google have also evolved special roles for "idea scouts" and "idea connectors" who recognize the importance of social and professional networks and mine the intersections of those networks for innovative ideas that can be formalized (Whelan, Parise, DeValk, & Aalbers, 2011).

Assertive scanners systematically glean ideas and information from those sources and routinely debrief participants for what they learned. They also use specialized roles, very often internal and external consultants, who act as gleaners who bring new ideas into the organization and track the ideas moving around in it. For example, Microsoft, like several other large companies, is known for having multiple McKinsey consultants working on different projects across the organization, and they are recognized as useful carriers of knowledge across external and internal boundaries.

The rule of thumb in turbulent environments is that the source of a truly serious disruption will be contextual—from "out there" or "left field," using those expressions. An intentionally varied deep dive into a particular topic, supported by a large number of information sources, will yield rich contextual knowledge that surfaces weak signals and early warning signs that narrow, function-specific (for example, marketing) scans never produce. Skilled global risk managers like those at AIG, for example, are adept at reading, listening, and traveling broadly for insight. Scanning also is best when teams focus attention on specific knowledge areas and then pool what they learn.

Organizations have to employ analytic tools and technologies for supporting large-scale, deep scans, and a few caveats are appropriate about such support tools. The machine determines the message; the features and capabilities of the analytic tools will drive the quality and usefulness of what is presented. Data-mining software or tracking systems crunch tons of information, but the risk is that the algorithms used and analytic tools applied can shape scan results (McCann & Gomez-Mejia, 1990). The Government of Singapore is working diligently at creating proprietary scanning systems designed with these deficiencies in mind. These systems work hard at keeping the qualitative fine texture and feel of information, not just the quantitative metrics of information in multiple fields or domains of interest.

Whether a scan occurs continuously or just once a year as a lead-in to a strategic planning update makes a big difference in the amount and timeliness of the information acquired. Most of us read newspapers or online news services daily, and use feeds and pings to alert us to new information, but very frequent systematic deep scans are expensive and time consuming. Finding the right balance between frequency and effort depends on the conditions being experienced by each organization or ecosystem.

You can do a great job of selecting the information sources you want through new personal technologies, yet the reality is that most of those feeds and tweets and social network interactions you are relying on are second- or third-hand sources that have already been filtered and interpreted. The challenge is for you to personally engage with direct source information as much as you can. Hard to imagine accessing large amounts of diverse information and knowledge firsthand, yet there is nothing comparable to seeing, touching, and hearing something yourself.

The objective is to generate unfiltered information by increasing the number of firsthand engagements with events of greatest interest. You may read about Shanghai technology incubators, but it is totally different to personally visit several of them and talk with the managers and start-up companies in them. Outsourcing scanning to others may be efficient, but it carries huge risks by losing the texture of the reality.

Organizations have greater resources to engage in scanning in-house, but they also balance this with external sources of information through consultants, professional associations, and groups. For the organization, the challenge is to bring those sources together to create a coherent overall picture of the environment. This picture must include more than just its immediate operating environment and include larger contextual and macro-level social, cultural, economic, political, and technological dimensions. This same challenge is magnified for the ecosystem, such as a global supply chain or industry group. The task here is to actively engage networks of professionals and practice groups across the chain members to pool their operating and contextual information.

Finally, scanning should not be a centralized activity. Just about everyone and every group engages in scanning to some degree. It must take place across levels and functions within the organization, with the collective perceptions and knowledge being used closest to the place where a response is needed. The leadership role is to ensure that individuals, teams, and larger organization units are scanning as effectively as possible using solid tools and skills, then bringing the knowledge into an integrated strategic picture.

Sensemaking

Sensemaking means taking collected information and giving it meaning by identifying patterns of relationships and implications for the organization. It is also about prioritization—differentiating between things that are important from those that are not. At the simplest level, judgments are about good and bad, opportunity and threat. Such simplistic SWOT (strengths, weaknesses, opportunities, threats) assessments are part of the typical strategic planning processes of yore where flipchart pages are plastered on conference room walls. We find that such assessments bury the richness and texture of the patterns revealed.

Instead there is a move to deeper, contextualized, and analytically rigorous methods, some using very elegant mathematical algorithms extracted from the intelligence agencies, such as CIA and NSA, and versions of search models from Bing, Google, or Yahoo. Consider Wikipedia, for example, where a topic or idea is built and validated using the collective input of hundreds of individuals.

We know of few tools as powerful as scenarios for engaging multiple stakeholders in future-focused modeling of alternative plausible explanations of events and trends. Such modeling flows directly into developing and testing alternative responses to the futures scenarios developed, and articulating the specific knowledge, skills, and abilities required by each scenario.

The practice of building futures scenarios has also been taken to a high art form by companies such as Shell Oil, one of the earliest proponents of scenarios, and refined in terms of practices and methods by programs at Oxford University in the United Kingdom (Ramirez, Selsky, & van der Heijden, 2010; Wack, 1995). Visit Shell's website for detailed instructions on how to use scenarios to support strategic decision making (http://www.shell.com /static/public/downloads/brochures/corporate_pkg/scenarios /explorers_guide.pdf).

Exhibit 5.1 provides a snapshot of the steps in a modified scenarios development process that we have used with teams of executives for promoting their strategic thinking and linking to the knowledge management process.

As a case in point, TECO Energy Inc., held a series of cross-functional retreats where multiple teams were asked to consider the knowledge challenges associated with four alternative scenarios—a status quo future, a "green energy" future, an energy-challenged future, and a terrorist-threat future in which energy companies were targeted. Each team built out those scenarios using Shell Oil guidelines and then explored what new knowledge would be required and how that should be translated into specific new skills and competencies. The teams then challenged each other's work and assumptions. In the conversation mentioned in Chapter Four with Clint Childress, TECO's SVP for HR and Corporate Services, he recognized the role such exercises play by noting: "Leaders must have future focus and this is only accomplished through constant environmental scanning, encompassing all segments of the business—financial, customer and constituent needs, work environment needs (people and technology). They have to focus not only on their own areas of expertise, but all

**Exhibit 5.1. Scenario-Building Exercise
for Executive Teams**

- Develop detailed written scenarios of multiple alternative possible futures by noting:
  - Major types of events and occurrences taking place within the industry and larger society
  - Major interactions among the key driving forces and trends being observed
  - Key assumptions that you are making in constructing each scenario (These are critical and identify the basis for them.)
- Identify and describe the strategic implications— that is, the potential consequences and outcomes —of each scenario for your strategic goals and business strategies
- Identify the key knowledge challenges and gaps created by each scenario and express as specific new competencies, skills, and capabilities that will be required to meet those challenges
- Identify and begin estimating when and how those competencies, skills, and capabilities will be developed or acquired

segments in totality. Scenario building exercises keep us thinking flexibly and with fresh eyes."

Sensemaking is a group sport. There has been recognition for some time that there are such things as the "wisdom of crowds" (Surowiecki, 2004), "smart mobs" (Rheingold, 2002), and "socially distributed cognition" (Hutchins, 1995). How the composition and history of top management teams affect sensemaking has also been studied at length (Sull, 2009; Sutcliffe, 1994). We know that people process more information better, and learn and act on it more effectively when more than two of them engage in sensemaking.

Organizations fall victim to the same sensemaking difficulties as individuals and teams, but in addition have the challenges of scale to overcome. Information needs to be scanned and screened as close to the teams needing that knowledge to act. It becomes critical to create ways of not just sharing but synthesizing that information into an overall picture of what the larger organization is experiencing. That may be an impossible task within a large global enterprise, but we believe that a lot more creative thinking needs to occur about how to overcome the downside of scale. We find that boundary-busting interchanges of people and use of a common technology platform for sharing knowledge are invaluable. People are the carriers of ideas; thus, encouraging free movement of people is the best way for moving ideas through the organization.

Finally, we've stressed the role of industry groups and trade associations for generating ecosystem-level knowledge. Participating in group-based sensemaking activities like futures scenario building at an industry level is especially valuable for developing a shared vocabulary and understanding about issues. The collective goals at that level are to surface the assumptions in each others' mental maps and models, pool scanned information, and envision plausible outcomes under a variety of conditions. Those involved understand each other's likely unilateral responses and define areas for collaborative response, which builds preparedness and shortens reaction time.

Shaping

Shaping refers to a very underappreciated aspect of Being Aware. It is concerned with how the knowledge generated from the preceding processes is best organized and presented so that others can effectively understand and take action based on it. For example, just presenting data in tidy tables adds little value without interpretations of its implications for action. Voluminous tables, charts, verbal summaries, and death-by-PowerPoint presentations similarly bury important ideas. When Toyota Motor Company began seeing data about defects and parts problems in such models as its Camry, and anecdotal information about accidents began surfacing, it was a sensemaking failure to not connect the dots, but it was also a failure in the shaping process because that knowledge was not integrated and presented in ways that led to direct, immediate action. For information to become knowledge, it requires both meaning and shaping.

The challenge here is to agree on the best ways to offer and present information so that it is actionable knowledge, not just data (Fink & Vickers, 2011). Fields such as finance have well-developed analytics, but financial reports are also increasingly being supplemented with detailed narratives on a broader range of contextual issues such as corporate social responsibility (CSR) performance.

Sharing

KM practices for sharing knowledge have become very sophisticated and varied. They come in a variety of forms, ranging from company-wide proprietary and commercial technology platforms such as Share Point, to individual and group-based techniques such as communities of practice and best practices sharing. The core challenge here, of course, is the functionality of those methods in terms of putting current, rich, and accessible knowledge in the right place, at the right time, and for the right people. This challenge is well known and a topic of constant concern in a growing, knowledge-intensive global organization. The global management consulting firms such as McKinsey, Accenture, and Cap Gemini have struggled for over two decades to master this challenge.

Storing

Finally, the storing process focuses on the archiving of collected knowledge for ready access, reexamination, and reuse. There is a bias toward giving more credibility to the most recent information or knowledge generated, and in turbulent environments currency is critical. Nonetheless, there are simply too many stories about how "old" knowledge about an event, process, or person provides helpful perspective about an immediate issue or leads to unexpected major opportunities.

For example, Searle's recognition of aspartame as a sweetener was the result of an accidental lab incident when a Searle bench chemist licked a finger that happened to have aspartame on it. Aspartame already existed, having been created by a Japanese company, but Searle was exploring its use in ulcer treatment (McCann, 1990). The already accumulated knowledge about aspartame became invaluable for launching one of the most profitable food industry products in history.

Microsoft's Bill Buxton goes further by adding, "Anything that's going to have an impact over the next decade—that's going to become a billion-dollar industry—has always already been around for 10 years" (Thompson, 2011, p. 44). Even dusting off the historical accounts of European explorers traveling through Central Asia five hundred years ago has provided insight today about the location of rich ore and mineral deposits in Afghanistan. Stored knowledge has currency and accessing it efficiently and placing it in the right context with other knowledge is a valuable part of Being Aware.

Summary

Being High AR Aware means mastering the concepts, skills, practices, and processes associated with KM and OL. This is doable, although it requires commitment, effort, and resources.

Our interest in this chapter has not been describing ten tools or pressing for a specific knowledge management technology platform. Learning more about these is obviously important and there are rich literatures and readily available experts to help you do that.

Rather, our vital interest is building an appreciation of the role that the five awareness processes play in building AR. Agility and resiliency require sensitivity to larger environments, because it is the movement of ideas and events within them that drive rapid and disruptive change. The timeliness and richness of the knowledge presented to decision makers is critical in determining whether something becomes an opportunity, which tests agility, or a threat that impacts the organization, which unfortunately tests resiliency.

We have argued that the very outlines, dimensions, and content of an environment are shaped by the mental maps and models of individuals, teams, and organizations operating within it. Mindfulness is a virtue in this regard. It means creating the capacity for objectively and systematically exploring how the organization learns and manages what it knows. We have offered some concepts and models to support that exploration.

There are a few basic steps to take in this direction. The first step is to pay attention to the five Awareness processes just described and audit their effectiveness in your own organization. Examine how information and knowledge are acquired and whether the process is as representative of the organization's environment as it should be. This means exploring how ideas cross organization boundaries, enter, work around, and take hold in the organization. Social network analyses will reveal the key idea generators and entry points. It is fair to ask whether they are the right individuals and groups to be doing that as well as changes made to alter those flows.

We are particularly supportive of team- and group-based ways of creating shared appreciations of the environment, as they support group learning and knowledge sharing. For example, although they may seem a pointless exercise, annual planning processes can provide opportunities for individuals and groups to provide meaningful scanning input by asking questions such as: What are the four or five biggest ideas/issues/trends that you see growing over the next year that may impact us? What issues and trends should we be paying greater attention to that we presently seem to be missing? Nothing complicated, but the results can be powerful.

It is also important to revisit the three sources of active learning failure discussed earlier in the chapter. One challenge is to avoid overwhelming individuals with too much divergent, rich information that simply cannot be absorbed and used constructively. Continuous monitoring of information loads at the individual and team levels is important. There is a strong inherent tendency toward adding more information, coupled with a rising intolerance and inattention to it; too much information beyond some point is mind deadening rather than expanding.

This raises the question of whether the organization can identify, select, and develop individuals with highly developed qualities of active learners. Team-based capabilities can also be developed for scanning, sensemaking, and shaping information. We suggested that this is indeed not only possible but essential. Selection and development processes must target these skills and abilities. Once selected and developed, individuals and teams must also be supported by organization-level tools and practices that reinforce Being Aware.

chapter
SIX

Designing for Action

I t is often not clear what element in a turbulent environment requires a response, or what response to make. Fortunately, the metrics and methods for matching the environment with effective responses are well developed in such fields as competitive intelligence, political risk assessment, and strategic issues management. The World Economic Forum (WEF), for example, has recently launched a Global Risk Network composed of a cross-sector "community of experts" who are dedicated to "learn, plan, and act jointly" around identified global risks, specifically to foster systemic resilience (Schwab, 2011, p. 56). A related Risk Response Network (RRN) aims "to provide private and public sector leadership with an independent platform to better monitor, prepare for, respond to and mitigate global and systemic risks" (www.weforum.org/community/risk-response-network). The government of Singapore also maintains a very sophisticated environmental scanning process within its Horizon Scanning Centre (HSC) that uses proprietary software to sense early-stage issues across seven domains, such as maritime security and food security (http://app.hsc.gov.sg/public/www/home.aspx).

This chapter is not about the specific tools and techniques used in those fields. If an organization meets opportunities and threats poorly, it is likely *not* due to a failure of tools and techniques. Instead, we focus on the underlying design principles and concepts for Being Action-Oriented, as we believe these provide the adaptive mindset needed to master turbulence. Being Action-Oriented and being open to change are closely related. Being open to change featured prominently among the high-performing organizations in our earlier AMA/HRI research. This has also been found consistently by other management researchers to be a key change attribute.

The popular expression for this assertive orientation is "forward leaning." The television network MSNBC uses this expression in describing a political action orientation. We use it to describe a decided bias toward reflective and premeditated action. This proactive orientation should drive an organization's engagement with its environment, to deploy its individuals and teams to seize advantage, leverage, and prepare. It should also drive an ecosystem's engagement with *its* environment for the same reasons, although this may be harder to visualize. This requires mobilizing the other capabilities examined up to this point. That is, Being Action-Oriented requires a clear, shared, and aligned sense of purpose and attention to wellness that assures stamina and persistence during change initiatives that may roll out over a very long period. It also requires the refined knowledge management and organizational learning skills and practices for acting with the right priorities on the right targets.

Key Features of Being Action-Oriented

Being Action-Oriented for High AR organizations means:

- Focusing and actively managing their cultures and tightly linking strategies to them
- Supporting active learning and knowledge management targeted to their major challenges

- Fostering an aggressive goal orientation and proactive posture for meeting those challenges
- Adopting an adaptive design mindset focused on combining and recombining their special capabilities as conditions change
- Strategically managing boundaries for advantage and risk management

Focusing and Actively Managing the Culture

New research is confirming the vital linkage between organization strategy and identity, values, and beliefs (Dewhurst, Harris, & Heywood, 2011; Institute for Corporate Productivity, 2011). In its 2011 survey contrasting higher and lower performing organizations, the Institute for Corporate Productivity (i4cp) noted: "Strategies are more consistent, clearly communicated and well thought out in high performing organizations. They are more likely than other companies to say that their philosophies are consistent with their strategies, and their performance measurements mirror their strategies" (i4cp, 2011, p. 3). In our terms, this means that an organization's consistent purposeful actions produce a culture that buttresses its strategy, and this combination enhances performance.

To earn this performance dividend, the linkage between culture and strategy must be tight; however, this tight fit can also have a dark side when the culture rests upon poorly aligned values and beliefs that corrode commitment and turn employee behavior toward self-protection or self-aggrandizement. The result can be organization practices that disrupt progress toward goals and destroy value. Such was the case in Enron, as Alan Warnick, Enron's former VP for Organization Development and Training, has noted in an extensive published interview (Madsen & Vance, 2009) and in long conversations with one of us.

Alan left the company before its descent and collapse, and now happily resides at Utah State University. He related how the merging of InterNorth Corporation and Houston Natural Gas that created Enron in 1985 began an astoundingly fast development of values and beliefs built around Jeff Skilling and Ken Lay which eventually undid the company and its accounting firm, Arthur Andersen LLP. Those values and beliefs created a supercompetitive, toxic identity and culture expressed in deceptive and ethically questionable business practices and market strategies. Curiously, Joseph Berardino, Arthur Andersen's former CEO, offered a different slant in an interview on CNBC on December 2, 2011, the tenth anniversary of the Enron collapse. He asserted that "Good people do bad things under pressure" (Berardino, 2011). This may be true, but what does such a statement mean when the people involved were creating the pressure themselves, and *on* themselves? To us, this only reinforces our points in Chapter Four about the psychological toll of turbulence on people.

Tales of corporate mischief, incubated in toxic corporate cultures, did not start with Enron, of course. Robert Jackall put his finger on the underlying dynamic of a compromised ethical culture in his 1988 book called *Moral Mazes: The World of Corporate Managers*. This dynamic can be found—and loudly declaimed by the Occupy Movement—on Wall Street and in the U.S. banking system during the Great Recession, and has been the subject of several recent exposés. Indeed, the title of the Susan Madsen and Charles Vance interview with Alan Warnick is "Unlearned Lessons from the Past: An Insider's View of Enron's Downfall" (Madsen & Vance, 2009). And the collapse of MF Global under the watch of former U.S. Senator Jon Corzine is still unfolding as we write this chapter. The list of dysfunctional tight linkages between strategy and culture continues to grow.

Supporting Active Learning and KM

We noted in Chapter Five how the capability for Being Aware is built when KM and OL practices and processes are refined.

Designing and sustaining effective knowledge management processes, supported by deliberate organizational learning practices for scanning, sensemaking, shaping, sharing, and storing knowledge, are valuable competencies. Organizations like McKinsey, Cap Gemini, Accenture, and others know their primary competitive asset is the knowledge they possess and create for and through others.

From an action oriented perspective, KM has to be tightly focused to marshal thinking and action around the key knowledge challenges facing the organization. A case in point is Microsoft's decision to exploit cloud computing as its next major market thrust, when much of its earlier product history was based in PC desktop software. The new cloud initiative will demand new knowledge and skills. How quickly Microsoft is able to identify, build, and roll these up into a new set of competencies and capabilities are critical action-orientation challenges.

Another example at an ecosystem level is the U.S. auto industry's voluntary decision to go along with the new federal 54.5 mpg fleet standard by 2025. This standard is likely to create a whole new set of knowledge challenges for the automakers. How well they can build capabilities around those challenges could decide their competitive futures.

Developing KM and OL processes are critical, but making sure they identify and focus on specific strategic knowledge challenges in a sustained way is just as critical. It is those knowledge challenges around which you build, bundle, and leverage new capabilities. This requires a level of discipline and commitment that the most innovative global companies understand fully.

Fostering an Aggressive, Proactive Posture

It is notable that the same high-performing organizations we found in our earlier research are also aggressive about initiating change that furthers their goals (AMA/HRI, 2006; i4cp, 2010).

Figure 6.1. Organization Postures Toward Change

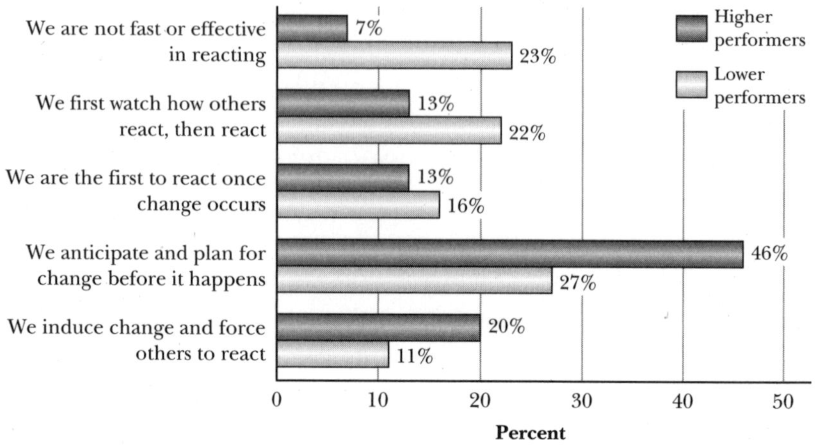

Source: American Management Association/Human Resources Institute (AMA/HRI), 2006.

Figure 6.1 summarizes the different postures or orientations to different change strategies. You can see that the high performers in terms of financial performance and competitiveness reported that they anticipate and proactively plan for change before it happens, or they actually induce it and force others to react, at almost twice the rate that lower-performing organizations reported. This is a proactive posture that can be fostered by helping individuals and teams to see environmental trends as opportunities. It also means removing barriers to action so that employees can take initiative and seize potential opportunities. In contrast, lower performers likely see external trends as threats, promoting a problem-centered mentality.

One of the dangers of complex, many-layered organizational structures is that individuals and teams have difficulty thinking like proprietors. They lack understanding or commitment to the business, its business model (that is, how it makes money), and its performance goals. Southwest Airlines has fought this; it trains its flight attendants, booking agents, pilots, and crews to understand each other's jobs and responsibilities and how they relate to shared performance metrics, such as ground turnaround time.

Another example is often found in technology-intensive companies like Microsoft. Their highly talented software designers are technically educated and technically focused in their work —sometimes to a fault. Many of those young designers need to appreciate much earlier in their careers how the products and services they develop actually have to make money—that is, how the company's business model really works and what their role is in it. Although some of them have even owned their own businesses or have a crystal-clear understanding of how to monetize intellectual capital, more need to build that knowledge and competence if the company is to keep up with market opportunities.

Creating an Adaptive Design Mindset

We advocate thinking about the capability we call Being Action-Oriented from an adaptive design perspective. This perspective is a departure from traditional thinking about organization design based on power/authority, division of labor, and hierarchical relationships. We know that a structural choice of a functional, product, geographic, or matrix design is an important reflection of how an organization fundamentally postures itself toward its environment (Galbraith, 2009; Kesler & Kates, 2010). However, thinking about design solely in terms of making a structural choice misses the essence of adaptive designing for High AR.

Because turbulent environments demand continuous development of all the capabilities noted in this book, adaptive design choices need to be viewed the same way. It is limiting to talk about organization *design* as something that, once done, remains in place for some period. It is more accurate to talk about organization *designing* as a continuous process. In this line of thinking, design is a verb, not a noun.

For example, the problem with hierarchical structures is that they quickly become overloaded with information as turbulence increases. This slows decision making. Aaron Wildavsky recognized this danger in this process two decades ago in talking about the increased risk exposure of centralized organizations: "The larger and more centralized the organization that seeks to predict the future, the longer it will take to get agreement, the fewer hypotheses it can try, and the more costly each probe is likely to be. . . . Decentralized anticipation (numerous independent probes of an uncertain future) can achieve a greater degree of safety" (Wildavsky, 1988, p. 8).

The reliance on hierarchical structures is excessive across the corporate landscape, and such traditional structures are increasingly being challenged. Everyone's favorite advocate for action orientation is Tom Peters (remember "ready, fire, aim"?), a vocal and determined enemy of "structure" through such books as *Liberation Management: Necessary Disorganization for the Nanosecond Nineties* (1992) and the earlier *Thriving on Chaos: Handbook for a Management Revolution* (1987).

Despite considerable work on such alternatives, management scholars have yet to find forms of organization that are equally effective as traditional hierarchies in organizing Microsoft's one hundred thousand regular employees, plus one hundred thousand contingent employees, across five continents. Structure serves many purposes. It provides stability and a degree of certainty (Huy & Mintzberg, 2003). It can be a source of identity for employees and managers because it defines boundaries—between groups, between specialties, between divisions, between the organization and the environment.

An adaptive design mindset does mean questioning structure. In the most general sense, structure is nothing more than patterns of recurring relationships over time. These relationships may be between people, teams, or even processes and ways of doing things within the organization. At the simplest level, a job held by one individual is a collection of tasks and associated responsibilities all accomplished using specific knowledge, skills, and abilities. At a team level, the same is true, and at the organization level teams get joined into business units, and business units into divisions, and so forth.

Designing Around Strategic Capabilities. Designing is based upon the recognition and development of the unique capabilities of individuals, teams, and organizations along with the refinement of the integrating and delivery processes required for those capabilities to have maximum impact. Designing also occurs at the ecosystem level when alliances, joint-ventures, federations, and multi-industry consortiums are created, reworked, and disbanded to deal with industry- or sectorwide opportunities and threats as they rise and fall. The WEF and its Global Risk Network, mentioned at the beginning of this chapter, is a good example. Designing is a continuous, dynamic process of matching capabilities at all levels to conditions that emerge in highly turbulent environments through an organization's strategies.

Our perspective about designing an organization around its capabilities is not new. Indeed, the academic literature regarding strategic capabilities and dynamic capabilities has been growing for some time (Birkinshaw & Gibson, 2004; Coff & Kryscynski, 2011; Eisenhardt & Martin, 2000; Sirmon, Hitt, & Ireland, 2007). This work sprang in part from what strategy researchers call the resource-based view (RBV) of organizations, which evolved from work in the 1980s about how distinctive competencies can be a source of competitive market advantage (Barney, 1991).

The basic premise of the capabilities research is that specific kinds of capabilities, representing unique groupings of competencies and skills, can be identified, selected, developed, and harnessed in unique ways that generate competitive advantage and greater firm performance. The key processes have been called "structuring, bundling and leveraging" (Sirmon et al., 2007).

The search is on for what these unique capabilities may be. Some of this research has raised questions about how specific capabilities such as "absorptive capacity"—the ability to absorb large amounts of information and effectively use it to advantage—support adaptation in "high velocity" environments (Eisenhardt & Martin, 2000). The current focus, which should be gratifying for HR professionals, is on the organization's unique "human capital" as a key capability. The capabilities associated with selecting, developing, and engaging a workforce appear to be an even more critical source of competitive advantage than first recognized (Coff & Kryscynski, 2011).

Roll-Up/Rollout Capabilities Model. From a capabilities perspective, you can think about the structures of relationships at all the levels discussed previously as bundles of capabilities that are, in turn, composed of competencies which are, in turn, composed of specific, unique combinations of knowledge, skills, and abilities. Ultimately, that knowledge and those skills and abilities derive from the cognitive and developmental experiences of individuals. Capabilities are in our view "rolled-up" sets or bundles of these constituent building block elements.

The design challenge is to recognize which capabilities must be created and designed using these constituent building blocks, given the knowledge challenges and environmental conditions facing the organization. These capabilities are then "rolled-out" as part of a strategy intended to produce desired outcomes. If any of these building blocks are weak or missing, they must be aggressively developed or acquired and brought to a keen edge so that they can then be combined and integrated with others in ways that fully meet the organization's knowledge challenges and environmental conditions. Figure 6.2 illustrates the cycle of activities associated with this process of rolling up and rolling out capabilities.

Figure 6.2. The Capabilities Design Cycle

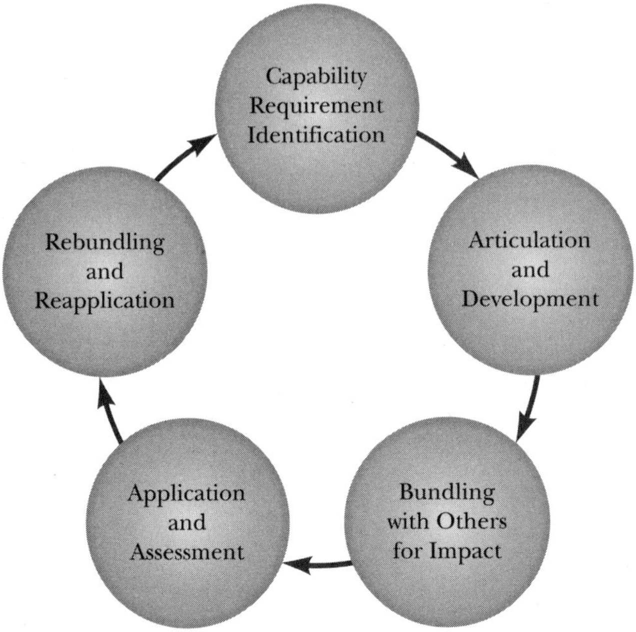

Figure 6.3 illustrates in a simple way how this design process would look for a specific strategy. In this roll-up/rollout model, there are specific bundles of cognitive and developmental experiences at the individual level that are expressed as knowledge, skills, and abilities at individual and team levels, These knowledge, skills, and abilities are then bundled into competencies and into capabilities that are rolled out in support of a global, open innovation strategy that generates localized products across various international markets.

To understand how those capabilities are defined and best expressed, let's take another example. Every organization makes a choice about its leading edge or dominant contact point with its various markets. For multibusiness companies like Microsoft,

Figure 6.3. Roll-Up/Rollout Capabilities Design Model

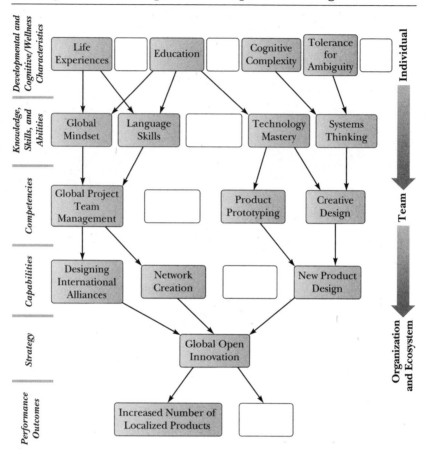

the business unit with its many product teams is that edge. Microsoft recognized some time ago that the corporate level could never stay in close enough contact with customers in so many different, dynamic businesses. The corporate level may be where overall governance and global resource allocation choices are made, and so those governance and allocation capabilities are highly refined at that level. But the business unit or division is Microsoft's clear choice for customer engagement as that is where the business and environment interact most intensely and directly.

This, then, is the point where the appropriate product and customer engagement capabilities are bundled and leveraged.

This designing process based on rolling out capabilities can be very organization specific. Patrick Pichette, Google's CFO, eschews formal business units because they create resource allocation and turf issues that he believes can be mitigated by using collaborative decision-making processes that cut across product areas (Manyika, 2011). Let's see how that design choice may change as Google doubles and triples in size. There are already signs that Google's proliferation of products is creating rivalries—not necessarily a bad thing, of course—that look and sound similar to classic business division battles in more mature and bigger organizations (Levy, 2011).

Adaptive designing is therefore about finding the best, most unique bundles of capabilities that best match the opportunities and response demands of an organization's environment through well-articulated strategies. This involves continually aligning and making trade-offs among four moving parts: sets of desirable cognitive and developmental characteristics; knowledge, skills, and abilities; competencies; and strategy-focused capabilities. Different choices each have advantages to be maximized and disadvantages to be minimized.

We see a decided preference today in favor of more dynamic, flexible structural configurations that engage and integrate many stakeholders. We also support engaging ecosystem partners to collaboratively respond to shared issues. From the point of reference of the organization, this participation is both horizontal (across the organization) and vertical in two directions—down the organization to individuals and teams, and up and out into its ecosystem (Lawler & Worley, 2011). Stuart Hart, in *Capitalism at the Crossroads* (2010), talks about engagement as "fanning out" to incorporate more divergent thinking from stakeholders and "fanning in" to integrate that knowledge into forceful response initiatives.

Strategically Managing Boundaries

In Chapter Two we discussed the idea that boundaries have come to be seen as "problems," a view emanating from what we called the dominant logic of open systems thinking, which was rampant during the 1980s and 1990s. This view is still prevalent now, although seasoned by the reality that boundaries can be useful to contain disruptive change and severe shocks, whether environmental, social, economic, or political.

This dual good/bad nature of boundaries deserves much closer attention. We believe *strategic boundary management* (SBM) is one of the most important and least understood features of Being Action-Oriented for High AR. This is intriguing because boundary management is a fundamental, ongoing, ever-present activity at individual, team, organization, and ecosystem levels (Bacharach, Bamberger, & McKinney, 2000; Delapierre & Mytelka, 1998; Ernst & Chrobot-Mason, 2011; Hirschhorn & Gilmore, 1992). Cynthia Kurtz and David Snowden of IBM go so far as to claim that: "Boundaries are possibly the most important elements in sense-making, because they represent differences among or transitions between the patterns we create in the world we perceive" (2003, p. 474).

In broad terms, boundary management involves what Bacharach, Bamberger, and McKinney (2000) call "tactics actors use to maintain, guard, or expand their boundaries to open, close or expand their self vis-à-vis the other" (p. 706). Monty Lynn (2005), borrowing from J. D. Thompson's 1967 classic work on organizational behavior, refers to boundary management as a process of dynamically buffering the organization to balance the need for external adaptability and change with a corresponding need for internal stability and order.

Like knowledge management and organizational learning, SBM is a powerful frame-shifting perspective. It asks you to mindfully and systematically assess the risks and value of all your relationships—that is, interdependencies—and decide which ones should be strengthened, sustained, or ended. When a relationship is valuable, SBM requires that it also be actively managed in terms of its risks and costs.

We would argue that Arthur Andersen did not actively manage the risks and costs in its relationship with Enron, and this led to Andersen's downfall. Partnership structures are inherently inadequate for dealing with financial costs of the magnitude that Andersen had to face because of poor boundary management between itself and its clients, and between one part of its operations and the rest of the partner-based operations in other regions. The damage, once felt, could not be readily contained. Similarly, AIG did not manage its boundaries very well when its insurance business was backing risky derivative products peddled by the big investment banks. True, it did not collapse, but it fell to the federal government to make a difficult, expensive decision about whether AIG was "too big to fail."

SBM may feel like what we have called "social triage," in which winners like AIG are separated from losers like Lehman Brothers in a brutal lifeboat survival exercise (McCann & Selsky, 1984). However, SBM is immensely valuable for clearing obstacles, generating new degrees of freedom, and speeding action. This means accepting a minimal amount of structure between work units and hierarchical levels, recognizing the negative consequences of the mental and operational boundaries present. Even a living cell has boundaries; they buffer the cell's internal functions from external disturbances. At the same time those boundaries must be permeable enough for the cell to import and export energy. The combination of buffering and permeability enables the cell to function as an integral organism. Similarly, the task in an organization is to provide sufficient boundaries to give individuals and work groups an identity, but keep them focused outward, rather than inward.

An agile organization may seek minimal boundaries, whereas a resilient organization needs to create and defend boundaries to protect and preserve its core identity and purpose. The drives for agility and resilience must find a balance in terms of managing costs and risks inherent in its interdependencies. In the wake of the past decade's accounting scandals and the Great Recession, boundaries are being quickly formed and defended between companies and auditors, boards and management, credit rating agencies and client companies. We consider strategic global risk assessment to be a form of boundary management. It is becoming standard across many industries, and multi-organizational bodies, such as the WEF mentioned earlier, support those efforts. The state of the art, however, has a long way to go in linking risk assessments to risk management controls and action plans.

We believe that SBM consists of strategies, actions, and processes that an organization uses to manage its critical external relationships by thoughtfully, selectively, and systematically: (a) destroying or minimizing boundaries that have been previously built, (b) forming new boundaries between itself and others where none previously existed, and (c) defending existing boundaries. Each of these three generic strategies—destruction, formation, and defense—requires explanation. Table 6.1 illustrates these strategies and examples of what an organization could do in each case in terms of three kinds of practices and skills.

Boundary Destruction. An organization destroys boundaries internally when combining business or work units, or delayering levels of management. The persistent theme has been to work against boundaries with a vengeance. Anything that slows internal decision making and change initiatives is to be challenged, a potential target for elimination.

An organization also destroys boundaries between itself and others in its environment when it initiates new relationships and exchanges such as partnering, joint ventures, strategic alliances, and mergers and acquisitions. Many of these initiatives create new interdependencies and risks that must be managed and they are far from cost free. There is growing evidence that outsourcing is

Table 6.1. Strategic Boundary Management Strategies and Practices

Strategy	Objective	Normative Practices and Skills	Operational-Technical Practices and Skills	Physical-Spatial Practices and Skills
Boundary Formation	Create boundaries to minimize or eliminate low-value or disruptive interdependencies.	Emphasize new differences in values, beliefs, and ends or goals to differentiate identities.	Build computer firewalls; form trade coalitions with strict membership requirements.	Locate in a secure office park; form checkpoints and other movement controls.
Boundary Defense	Enforce existing boundaries to preserve and protect existing valued interdependencies.	Reinforce existing differences and similarities in values, beliefs, and ends or goals.	Create operating procedures to govern current relationships; enforce security agreements.	Colocate with current partners; restrict current open borders to neighboring states.
Boundary Destruction	Reduce significance or eliminate existing boundaries to create new interactions and exchanges with external environment.	Emphasize similarities in values, beliefs, and ends or goals to create basis for trust and shared identity.	Engage in outsourcing and create integrated supply chains; form new regional trade agreements.	Locate offices in urban center with free flows of people; create shared facilities with partners.

creating some serious customer service problems for some organizations and proving more costly than anticipated (Aron & Singh, 2005). As a result, companies such as Dell Computer have pulled some off-shored/outsourced activities back internally. Global supply chains are also being "hardened" in an attempt to better manage the number and resiliency of the many nodes along the entire supply chain (Sheffi & Rice, 2005).

At an ecosystem level, consider the case of international trade agreements such as NAFTA and successive rounds of WTO trade negotiations. Destruction of global trade barriers has clearly benefited many. However, entire populations have become economically and politically destabilized by boundary destruction in the form of reductions or total eliminations in tariffs and trade restrictions.

The costs and risks associated with increasing openness and interdependence through boundary destruction have not been sufficiently appreciated. This is not intended as an argument for decoupling and closing off an organization from its environment. Obviously, an organization can never be, nor should be, completely open or closed, despite the call for "boundaryless organizations" (Delapierre & Mytelka, 1998). Boundary destruction makes sense—up to a point. Recognizing and strategically managing that balance is the challenge.

Boundary Formation and Defense. Boundary formation and defense are essential, complementary strategies to boundary destruction. We are advocating more than a simple, intuitive threat-reflex reaction, and we are *not* promoting a retreat or general closing-off of organizations from "foreign entanglements." The United States government will realistically never be able to defend its boundaries completely against all threats, despite best efforts. Steel walls along the Mexican border won't do it. Nor can any organization do any better.

What we are advocating is the selective, deliberate use of formation and defense strategies to provide temporary stability until additional capacity is built or the likelihood of disruption recedes. Today's organizations are not medieval monasteries or walled fortresses, but their boundary management skills need developing as the potential for disruption due to turbulence increases.

Boundary formation has as its objective the selective elimination, or reduction in intensity, of some existing interdependencies to reduce the costs and risks associated with them. Relationships and exchanges are examined in terms of their value to the organization relative to the costs and risks they pose, and then conscious choices are made to either reduce their significance or completely end them. An outsourcing relationship, for example, can be terminated and the outsourced activities recaptured within the organization, or at least placed near-shore rather than off-shore (Koerner, 2011).

Boundary defense has as its objective the selective management of existing high-value interdependencies to optimize and preserve their value to the organization. Existing boundaries are managed more actively and intensively. Boundary defense means making tough choices, essentially deciding that this relationship is important but that other one is not. It means saying "no"—the costs and risks simply do not merit maintaining that relationship, or it should not be expanded any further, or additional resources should not be allocated to managing it. It involves consciously protecting the organization from external disruption through what we might call "relationship triage."

Finding the creative and dynamic tension between the three core SBM processes—boundary destruction, boundary defense, and boundary formation—is the critical challenge in turbulent environments (Lynn, 2005). Many organizations have been very good at destroying boundaries internally and externally in their drive for agility, but they need to develop boundary formation and defense capabilities as equally critical for resiliency. Boundary formation and defense serve as both short-term and long-term strategies for protecting, focusing, and channeling available adaptive capacity.

Implications for Being Action-Oriented

Organizations must simply become better at building, sustaining, and applying High AR capabilities. In this chapter we have argued the need for organizations to develop their entire set of agility and resiliency capabilities and to adopt a designing mindset for applying them more strategically. This is no small challenge. New investments in areas where costs may have been driven out— training and development, for example—will have to be increased. At first blush this may be difficult to justify, but senior HR executives must make the case for investments that directly and measurably support Being Action-Oriented.

If most everything is variable and open to change, then this means that individuals, teams, business units, and functions need to develop strong change management skills. Change management can become a core competence in itself—see our work on continuous change thinking and the use of scenarios (Selsky & McCann, 2008). The knowledge and skills for effective change management are well known and can be developed. We have been pleased to see, for example, how well M&A transition and integration management skills have evolved over the past twenty years. When the integration of a large, important acquisition can be done quickly and effectively, it saves millions of dollars and increases market impact. Our point is that change management as a core competence means that your organization should strive to be the most highly advanced and sophisticated in this regard. Change management can become a potent source of competitive advantage in a turbulent environment, just as much as a superior operating process or product design feature can be.

The danger that lurks here is that a change-capable organization might be tempted to induce so much change that it leads to chaotic internal conditions that destabilize everyone connected to it, including customers. To avoid this danger we advocate three things. First, change needs to be guided by vision and purpose, but the change process itself needs a GPS unit—a conceptual framework or model that helps you understand what happens if a particular change is made, and what to do next. There are several such models around, such as the time-tested "star" model of organization design first developed by Jay Galbraith in the 1970s (Galbraith, 1995) or, still one of our favorites, the McKinsey 7-S model in its original and subsequent variations (Peters & Waterman, 1982). Which model to use is almost beside the point; but you do need a model to serve as a guide.

Second, you need to become very good at reading the change pulse of the organization and its environment (Huy & Mintzberg, 2003). Are you moving so fast that the company's pulse is racing dangerously, or so slow that the company is lethargic and slow to respond? As Shona Brown and Kathleen Eisenhardt (1998) note in their book *Competing on the Edge: Strategy as Structured Chaos,* rhythm counts, and being able to set the pace and rhythm of change is important. Andy Grove's predilection when he was running Intel was to "run the company scared"—a high pulse rate—to maintain a competitive edge by playing industry disruptor (Grove, 1996).

Third, High AR Action-Oriented organizations are good at recognizing that running at a persistently fast speed exacts a heavy toll on individuals and teams. Such organizations invest in other capabilities such as wellness programs to build agility and resiliency. They put reward and support systems in place to sustain the pace needed.

Finally, managing in a rapidly changing and disruptive world also means developing a more sophisticated appreciation and balanced approach to strategic boundary management. Strategically, this may mean electing to do something new alone, rather than extending alliances and partnering relationships when the risks are high or impossible to determine. Fundamentally it means appreciating the dynamic tension and trade-offs required between the benefits of greater openness and the costs and risks associated with greater interdependence. At a minimum, it means investing more effort and resources in strategic risk assessment and management. Operationally, an organization's SBM practices should be inventoried, their effectiveness assessed, and variety expanded to provide a full range of practices for any situation encountered.

chapter
SEVEN

Being Resourceful

B y this time it is clear that AR involves much more than simply acting fast to seize an opportunity or bouncing back from a damaging impact. The challenge we find for many organizations today is not just to act quickly, but also knowledgeably and effectively, with well-developed and focused capabilities. In this chapter we add to this challenge the requirement to also act creatively and innovatively. Being Resourceful demands entrepreneurial thinking and action at individual and team levels as well as differentiated innovative capacity at organization and ecosystem levels.

Our own research revealed that High AR organizations were adept at quickly deploying and redeploying resources in novel ways as conditions changed. The old admonition that there should be lots of slack resources to buffer the organization from external fluctuations was never a consideration; the day of slack anything has been over for many years. Organizations have learned for economic reasons to be creative and flexible in how their resources are used, but the added benefit is that thinking in terms of multiple uses or applications for the same resources can speed response time, helping both agility and resiliency.

Perhaps this sounds very much like Being Action-Oriented—it is, but really amped up. Many organizations can effectively deal with normal predictable change at an operational and competitive business pace. They have well-developed problem-solving routines for dealing with operational break-downs, new product roll-outs, competitive mergers and alliances, and so on. This is the normal noise we are all used to dealing with. These conditions and the routines for coping with them are very important to master, of course, but to achieve High AR in a turbulent environment you need more. We are most concerned about the surprises and shocks that create dramatically altered playing field conditions; they are pregnant with the potential for severe performance disruptions as well as great strategic opportunities. As discussed in earlier chapters, on 9/11 Southwest Airlines experienced a total grounding of all its planes like everyone else in the airline industry in North America, but afterward became the first airline back in the air. This is not a trivial example, as the aftermath of 9/11 drove several U.S. airlines into bankruptcy, whereas Southwest continued to consistently generate a profit. We attribute some of their High AR to their consciously and relentlessly Being Resourceful.

To describe this type of behavior, Cynthia Lengnick-Hall and Tammy Beck, two authors with as keen an interest in agility and resiliency as ours, arrived at the concept of "learned resourcefulness," which they defined as: "the accumulation of established and practiced behaviors for innovative program solving that result in heightened levels of ingenuity, inventiveness, and *bricolage* (the imaginative use of materials for previously unintended purposes)" (Lengnick-Hall & Beck, 2009, p.47). The reference to *bricolage* in their definition is worthy of a chapter in itself, but Claude Lévi-Strauss (1966) is credited with this powerful concept's origin, and others have further developed its application.

Lengnick-Hall and Beck add that such behaviors can become incorporated as parts of disciplined, creative problem-solving routines and response repertoires that organizations can rely on in a wide range of situations. This highlights the learning aspect of resourcefulness and hearkens back to our emphases on organizational learning (OL) and knowledge management (KM) in Chapter Five and adoption of an adaptive design mindset in Chapter Six.

Other authors have noted how an entrepreneurial stance toward managing is central to building and maintaining an organization's dynamic capabilities. As David Teece (2007) noted, dynamic capabilities are "the distinct skills, processes, procedures, organizational structures, decision rules, and disciplines . . . which undergird enterprise-level sensing, seizing, and reconfiguring capacities difficult to develop and deploy. Enterprises with strong dynamic capabilities are intensely entrepreneurial. They not only adapt to business ecosystems, but also shape them through innovation and through collaboration with other enterprises, entities, and institutions" (p. 1319).

Although Teece's explanation is insightful, it is still difficult to differentiate what does or does not contribute to Being Resourceful from such encompassing statements. We prefer instead to think of Being Resourceful as the creative assembly and use of individual, team, organization, and ecosystem capabilities and resources to act and react to events in the external environment. Such actions and reactions may require very short cycle times, often under high stress, whereas others may be at the scale of transformative change and take months or even years to actualize. All of those actions and reactions may be initiated in response to perceived opportunities or to prevent or minimize negative performance impacts.

As a result, Teece may advocate for "entrepreneurial managerial capitalism" or Peter Drucker for "systematic entrepreneurship" as the *modus operandi* for engendering corporate creativity and innovation, but it is far from a slam dunk for several reasons (Drucker, 1985; Teece, 2009). In this chapter we look at some of these reasons and offer specific recommendations for promoting resourcefulness across levels.

Creativity and Its Limits

The study of creativity has an ancient history and continues to fascinate us all. Arthur Koestler's *The Act of Creation* (1964) is credited as one of the most thorough studies of creativity in its many forms, yet even his over-seven-hundred-page treatise does not remove the mystery. We won't try to do so either, but we do recognize some important challenges associated with systematizing the creative process for high performance.

First, we have noted repeatedly that High AR is compromised by turbulence but is also the antidote for overcoming its effects. Turbulence creates pressure on all AR fronts. In Chapter Five we noted that OL and KM are fundamental to Being Aware, but rapid, disruptive change requires fast acquisition and absorption of information to create knowledge that can be put to immediate use. Fast cycle times increase the chance for error, and contrary to common myth, sustained intense pressure does not spark ingenuity and creativity, but suppresses it over time (Amabile, Hadley, & Kramer, 2007). We also discussed some of the consequences of sustained high-pressure stress environments in Chapter Four. Tales of Millennial creatives thriving late into the night on energy drinks in tight cubicles deny the toll taken on their creativity over a long period of time. Burnout lurks behind those racks of colorful cans and plastic bottles.

Second, an organization's innovative capacity is a function of its ability to exploit knowledge from a wide variety of internal and external sources (Brown & Eisenhardt, 1997; Lichtenthaler & Lichtenthaler, 2009). Exploiting knowledge is done through various communication channels and established routines and processes such as scanning. Many of these channels and activities span team, business, organization, and ecosystem boundaries. Yet all those channels and routines can be disrupted by turbulence unless religiously resourced, staffed, and connected to decision makers. For example, Regina Dugan is the director of the Defense Advanced Research Projects Agency (DARPA), which sponsors such incredibly ingenious devices ranging from nano-hummingbirds to hypersonic planes. She believes that the only ways to keep up with the pace of innovation in fields impacting U.S. security are such unconventional strategies as "crowdsourcing" and open innovation networking, possibly even allowing others to keep control of their intellectual property (Penenberg, 2011b). Being Resourceful at an ecosystem level means understanding the motivations and finding the incentives to evoke collaboration, including letting intellectual property reside where it needs to be.

Third, we find the literature about entrepreneurial management and corporate innovation almost monolithic in its emphasis on the one best way for an organization to be entrepreneurial or innovative. There is, or was, the "HP Way," or the "IBM Way," or just "the way we do things here." It is potentially very devastating to innovativeness that the "one best way" is thought to be ideally located within centralized and specific functional R&D units just an arm's length from senior management control. The persistent theme today, of course, is that the entire organization and every individual and team in it needs to think like a business creator.

We suggest that "one best way" approaches to creativity and innovation are no longer viable. Even venerable companies such as IBM and Hewlett-Packard have stumbled at times and have had to shift their thinking about innovation, prompting a profound questioning of purpose and identity. For IBM with its historically and notoriously regimented culture, the questioning process was successful and it embarked on a long transformative process that moved its center of gravity from computer products to "Smart

Planet" information services, among other services. Now looking at IBM's website and talking with several program directors at seminars and conferences almost gives an other-worldly experience, as compared with the company's past.

For HP, the path forward is less clear as we write this book in early 2012, now that Meg Whitman has assumed the CEO role. The willingness to shed businesses and spend $9 billion for U.K.-based Autonomy Corporation PLC, an infrastructure software company, looks like a path toward reimagining the company similar to IBM's transformation. Mind you, the Autonomy deal was launched before she arrived, but there is apparent willingness to stay the course with that deal. Whitman is great at asking probing questions, so we suspect that HP will be doing a lot of thinking about its future over the next year or so.

Despite apparent successes, they may be transitory. This, ultimately, is the pernicious threat of turbulence—the dust doesn't settle and the next re-imagining may be right around the corner, or around the world. Our central point is that turbulence generates variety and there need to be equally varied ways of enacting creativity and innovation (Teece, 2007). Even Joseph Schumpeter, father of the concept of creative destruction, recognized the need for continuous innovation in products, methods, and ways of thinking about economic activity (Schumpeter & Opie, 1934).

The primary targets in recent decades have been new products and services, obviously necessary to compete and succeed in a global marketplace. The productivity and process improvement push of the 1980s came on the heels of the great threat of Japanese products in North American and European markets, and generated significant improvements with the focus on operations and services.

New organizational forms such as multidimensional matrix structures and virtual collaborative networks are important design innovations that have enabled such global operating scale (Galbraith, 2009; Galbraith, Downey & Kates, 2002). In addition, we would argue that the emergence of global supply chains supported by sophisticated shared information technologies is arguably one of this century's most important advances in international economic development.

The point is that every aspect of the way we approach work and economic activity should be a target for creative thinking and innovation. We believe that this is now the case . . . except in one respect. Turbulence ratchets up the stakes—it requires you to creatively and innovatively approach *how* you create and innovate.

Probing minds to detect the neurological and biochemical bases for behaviors may be one such approach, as we described in Chapter Four. Excuse us if we remain slightly uncomfortable where this form of innovation is heading. On the one hand, improving your leadership skills by teaching you the elements of brain functioning can help you better attune to your employees dealing with turbulent conditions; this is clearly a positive application. On the other hand, we also know that market research companies are using neuroscience tools to unlock such deep life mysteries as why consumers crave the orange cheese dust that gel-coats your fingers when eating Cheetos (Penenberg, 2011a). Trivial? Not for one of the biggest brands in the world, and it is, after all, still a new field with lots of experimentation.

Four Innovation Scripts

The core implication of turbulence for Being Resourceful, expressed through creativity and innovation, is that it must be, well, resourceful. That is, it must take multiple forms at multiple levels depending on the situation at hand in order to truly promote agility *and* resiliency together. Turbulence creates a greater variety of conditions than more placid environments, and greater variety dictates equally varied responses. Some time ago Ross Ashby called this "the law of requisite variety" (Ashby,

1956). In a recent study of two hundred Dutch companies over two decades, Patrick Reinmoeller and Nicole van Baardwijk (2005) concluded that "focusing on one innovation strategy to the exclusion of others may produce innovation, but it will not lead to resilience" (Reinmoeller & van Baardwijk, 2005, p. 65). Like us, they advocate a dynamic balancing of *multiple* innovation strategies.

We call these differentiated responses or approaches innovation *scripts* that managers follow, or read from, given certain settings and cues. All four may be occurring simultaneously at different speeds, locations, and levels in your organization. Some involve individuals and teams acting entrepreneurially, whereas others engage the entire organization and other external actors in the ecosystem. Some scripts are helping you pursue perceived opportunities with entrepreneurial zeal, whereas others are helping solve problems creatively, preempting threats and minimizing damage. They are differentiated responses for creativity and innovation matched to the conditions encountered (Wilson & Doz, 2011).

The four primary scripts are summarized in Table 7.1. Although a 2×2 matrix is obviously very simplistic, we believe that this model is still powerful for framing your basic choices for matching responses to the conditions experienced. The two key dimensions for differentiating them are the *potential impact* or magnitude and the *time frame* required for a response.

Regarding the magnitude dimension, *low impact* means that some event or condition, though clearly calling for a response, does not pose a significant immediate opportunity or challenge at that time. *High impact* means that an event or condition poses significant performance implications for the organization and demands major commitment of attention, resources, and effort to manage it. This may be a major opportunity or a major threat demanding agile action to take advantage of, avoid, or ameliorate the event or condition.

Table 7.1. Four Creativity and Innovation Approaches

Speed of Response

	Short Time Frame	Long Time Frame
High Impact	**Fast Track Innovation Model** • Reactive change • Team project-level creative problem solving • Acting on events • Creative problem solving in a time-pressured context • Situational involvement based on knowledge and expertise • Active network support of effort • Example: *Apollo 13*	**Strategic Corporate Innovation Model** • Transformative change • Platform-level innovation • Acting on larger system structure • Formal roles, protocols, and established routines • High skill specialization and depth at unit level • Active network engagement to generate resources and knowledge • Example: Boeing Dreamliner
Low Impact	**Improvisational Innovation Model** • Spontaneous, real-time creative problem solving • Individual or team-based knowledge and skills primary • Stop-gap effort until more formal protocols and routines are established • Localized resources used at team or unit level • Limited network activation • Example: Arab Spring	**Routine Incremental Innovation Model** • Tactical change • Competitive opportunity or operational improvement driven • Well-established protocols and routines at business unit level • Business unit and functionally specific resources • Active network engagement • Example: Kaizen process in Toyota plant

Magnitude of Impact

Time frame refers to the speed of the required response. This dimension has become even more important over the past twenty years due to research on what are called "high-velocity" and "hypercompetitive" industries like the Internet and computer chip fabrication (Brown & Eisenhardt, 1997; D'Aveni, 1994). A short time frame means that the response must be immediate or rapid, whereas a long time frame means that the response may unfold over months or even years.

Low Impact/Long Time Frame— Routine Incremental Innovation

This innovation script is the stuff of normal opportunity recognition and entrepreneurial action. Most successful organizations are quite competent with this kind of creativity and innovation. Routine corporate innovation relies on established processes and protocols to bring forth ideas from research benches, client sites, and operating units, and then commercialize the most promising of these by shepherding them through the organization's value chain from engineering to sales. This script depends on budget lines and established teams and business units being in place to screen and launch new products and services, adjust operations, and respond to recognized patterns of competitive dynamics within an industry.

For global pharmaceutical companies like AstraZeneca, idea screening, drug design, clinical trials, and regulatory hurdles have largely been mastered. For a food company like Frito-Lay, tweaking a texture or flavor for an established product like Cheetos is more or less a routine process of innovating. Such routine innovation is designed to deal with market gaps and overlaps, product line extensions, competitive threats and streamlining operations through such improvements as global outsourcing. We call it routine because such practices spring from known knowledge, skills, and competencies rolled up into capabilities bundled in familiar ways at nearly all the leading knowledge-based companies in the world.

Despite calls for different ways of innovating and using alternative innovation scripts, much corporate innovation is still conducted in this well-established pattern. It is a familiar script and everyone knows their part. In terms of agility and resiliency, think "little A" and "little R." It is tactical innovation where advances and setbacks are real but manageable. Although increasingly expensive and less predictable in terms of outcomes, this corporate innovation model still dominates.

High Impact/Long Time Frame— Strategic Corporate Innovation

The problem with the preceding routine innovation model is that the competitive pace began speeding up in many industries. In *Hypercompetition*, a popular book in the 1990s on competitive strategy in fast-paced industries, Richard D'Aveni (1994) signaled a fundamental shift in rules of the competitive game. Innovate by disrupting the prevailing bases of competition in your industry, he said, or die. Clayton Christensen echoed this brutal advice in his advocacy for "disruptive technological change" (Christensen, 1997). This is the *strategic* corporate innovation model where agility requires a "big A" because it is critical for initiating change or at least staying in the race; and resiliency gets a "big R" because failure to absorb and counter the impact of a competitor's disruptive technology could lead to collapse.

The increasing magnitude of the opportunities, coupled with the potentially fatal consequences of failure, is leading to greater openness of the innovation process and more actors involved inside and outside the organization (Chesbrough, 2003). As Patrick Pichette, Google's CFO noted, "If we're not building a product that at least a billion people will use, we're wasting our time" (Manyika, 2011, p. 1). Strategic corporate innovation is a team sport played on a grand scale, unlike the tactical level innovation just described, which may be successful in wringing a few cents per item out of a production process.

Disruptive technologies such as the iPhone and Android operating systems can, for example, spell disaster for a company like Research in Motion (RIM) and its BlackBerry. RIM has adopted the Android platform for some new products as a response, but it is struggling to keep up on a platform basis. It isn't about a single product any longer, but innovation across an entire platform that services multiple future products. For Boeing, its Dreamliner passenger plane is financially a make-or-break product, but it is the new knowledge generated from innovative uses of composite materials like those in the Dreamliner that is giving Boeing a strong territorial claim over a whole range of future products.

Being Resourceful, High AR organizations recognize that in turbulent environments the conventional corporate innovation model described earlier, which works well at a tactical level, needs to be complemented with *strategic* innovation as the dominant model, which requires developing entirely new capabilities that are bundled and deployed in novel ways. Certainly, one lesson learned by Boeing is that it now knows how to play well with others through more than traditional joint-ventures and contractual arm's-length relationships. Their boundaries are being redrawn to incorporate new capabilities within global "innovation value chains" (Hansen & Birkinshaw, 2007; Santos, Doz, & Williamson, 2004) that include clusters of different actors with different specialized capabilities who are integrated within an overall innovation process. We provided an example earlier in this chapter of DARPA's opening up of its innovation process—a major game-changer in a procurement world noted for traditional contractual relationships.

This is the essence of "open innovation" (Chesbrough, 2003). For example, one organization may have highly developed design skills whereas another specializes in prototyping. All participate in thoughtfully configured ways to produce an outcome. In the next chapter, I talk about the special skills needed to support such value creation networks, or value constellations in the terminology of Normann and Ramirez (1993). It is worth reiterating here that greater openness carries greater risks, as well as rewards, in turbulent environments.

Low Impact/Short Time Frame— Improvisational Innovation

Opposite the high impact/long time frame strategic innovation script is one best associated with improvisation and real-time creative problem solving (Crossan, 1998). We cannot think of a topic that has received more attention in the management literature than creative problem solving and innovative thinking about new product design and development, and corporate intra- and entrepreneurship. A virtual tour through the Amazon and Barnes & Noble websites on these subjects could occupy you for days!

Why, then, are we dealing with these topics here? There are two main reasons. First, reacting to an event or condition very quickly may be necessary when it managed to get past your other awareness filters and processes; it evaded early detection in the scanning and sensemaking process and arrived on your doorstep demanding an immediate response. A competitor may have suddenly exited a hotly contested market and created an opportunity if you mobilize quickly. Can you do this? And if so, how? Or a powerful NGO announces that it detected a toxic effluent from one of your new supplier's plants in the Philippines. What do you do?

Actually, improvisation should not even be required in these kinds of situations. These questions should be easy to answer if you have well-established practices and protocols in place for handling them. But it is hard to foresee every contingency, so the alarm bells occasionally go off and the firefight begins. The danger here is that you may act so impetuously that you end up blowing the opportunity or creating an even bigger environmental mess than you otherwise would. Your actions turn out to be reckless in hindsight.

High-quality information is needed for effective sensemaking, that is, for forming accurate frames or definitions to describe encountered situations. Both examples just described are likely to seem chaotic at first and to contain ambiguous, perhaps even intentionally distorted information. Sensemaking also requires time, and that is sometimes missing when events slip past scanning and screening processes, or they are simply surprises that can never be anticipated, such as some natural disasters.

The second reason is that a situation may be so completely novel that it evades detection in your sensemaking filters. It may require additional time and attention to better understand and manage the situation using the other, more established innovation scripts. In other words, improvisation may be a stop-gap, buy-time solution more akin to triage than anything else. When you don't have polished practices and protocols in place, you can find yourself improvising until you can develop them well enough to take over.

Improvisation—the creative search for, structuring of, and development of novel solutions that respond quickly to real-time situations—is far from being an ad hoc and undisciplined process. It is not the same as brainstorming, although that may be a tool within it. To the contrary, it is based on specific assumptions, processes, and skills applied by individuals acting within a team. Although improvisation may rely on creative thinking skills and characteristics unique to some individuals and to team chemistry, the skills can be developed to build the reliability of the innovation process and quality of solutions generated (Crossan, 1998). In short, we are arguing that improvisation can be a deliberate innovation model, and a useful one for fostering agility and resiliency in a turbulent environment (Selsky & McCann, 2008).

Advertising agency TBWA/Chiat/Day and creative design firm IDEO have built phenomenally successful practices around what appears to be conceptual improvisation. One of us recalls participating in such a process with what was then Chiat/Day in its old Venice, California, warehouse offices. Displayed across a huge digital screen were sayings of a venerated Zen surfer guru such as "What if the sky were green and the sea were red?" or something close to that. The screen was designed to jog mindsets and stimulate creative juices, of course, but we observed that responses to a prospective client were paced, practiced, and productive. They also won the business in the case observed! Nothing has changed with TBWA. It's still quirky and fun.

IDEO is another poster child for practiced creative thinking. Tom Kelley and Jonathan Littman have effectively championed IDEO's approaches to creative design and demonstrated how these are thoughtfully considered and constructed to build reliability and quality (Kelley & Littman, 2001, 2005). Staffers may leave IDEO and go to work somewhere else for a while, only to return with new skills and ways of doing things that further refine the IDEO creative process.

Improvisation skills are best developed at individual and team levels, but those individuals and teams may increasingly reside across boundaries. As we note in Chapter Eight, technology-mediated networks bring ideas into and around the organization in ways impossible in the days of hotel weekend retreats and walls plastered with flipchart paper. Howard Rheingold's *Smart Mobs: The Next Social Revolution* (2002) is a reminder that there are lots of fresh perspectives and ideas outside the organization waiting to be used. The technology-mediated Egyptian uprising centered in Tahrir Square is a superb example of social improvisation. The key point is that you shouldn't and don't need to isolate your "creatives" by concentrating them in single departments or single teams.

High Impact/Short Time Frame— Fast-Track Innovation

The final innovation script captures the fast-track project team or multiple teams working in parallel to resolve big, immediate problems. Think of movies like *Apollo 13* rather than academic book citations for some of the most vivid examples of this script. In this movie, directed by Ron Howard, a lunar space capsule gets into trouble and the astronauts must work with NASA ground personnel to find solutions or die in space. We have effectively used this movie with executive groups on multiple occasions to extract characteristics of agile and resilient individuals, teams, and organizations.

What is most notable about this innovation approach is that it relies on practiced, disciplined problem solving that is heavily resourced and supported. It is *not* improvisation, however. It is team based, with individual members having the right skills and goal motivation, and the team integrally linked into the organization for whatever information, resources, and additional decision-making support that may be needed.

At times it appeared that the operators of the Fukushima nuclear plant were practicing improvisation during the seemingly imminent meltdown of reactors following the 2011 earthquake and tsunami. We argue they were not. They were connected into Tokyo Electric Power Company (TEPCO, the owner of the plant), national-level regulators, an international network of experts and resources, and were drawing on well-rehearsed protocols and crisis-management practices. Unfortunately, the magnitude and novelty of the conditions being generated threatened to overwhelm all of these protocols. This further threatened to push the operators toward improvisation, which was a dangerously inappropriate innovation script for such a large-magnitude situation. The problem with improvisation is that although it can be productive, it sometimes fails.

Organizations can get very good at fast-track crisis management when they are able to seriously question mindsets, expectations, and assumptions. The teams on the front line of innovation need to be reflective and have a strong learning orientation so that errors are caught, understood, and not repeated. Operational and logistics failures do get overcome in the face of natural disasters, and food safety scares do get quickly resolved, saving lives. This innovation script is tested, known, and works when it is intensely practiced and supported (Mitroff, 2002; Mitroff & Alpaslan, 2003). We therefore think that this should be the dominant innovation model in turbulent environments and for responding to very challenging, overwhelming events.

The crafted, practiced responses in this script should not be confused with the ritualized thinking and behavior characteristic of the Routine Incremental model. There are far too many examples where "tried-and-true" established ways of dealing with novel situations have led to disaster. Recall another movie, *Thirteen Days*, which vividly details the events and thinking associated with the 1962 Cuban Missile Crisis. It is based in part on the analysis of those events by Graham Allison and Philip Zelikow in *Essence of Decision: Explaining the Cuban Missile Crisis* (1999). If anything, the book and movie illustrate the dangers of approaching high-impact situations with unquestioned doctrinaire thinking. Need we mention the Iraq War?

Improving Resourcefulness

Being Resourceful means facing two immutable facts for mastering turbulence. First, following Ashby's law of requisite variety, you must approach variety with variety. In this case, all of the uncertain, richly connected, and complex situations you encounter cannot be approached the same way. The four innovation scripts we've described are archetypes—relatively simple models designed to convey just some of the response varieties possible.

Second, we noted how it is not desirable to bottle up creativity and innovation in one business unit or a small number of research teams when dealing with turbulent environments. Understandably, on the one hand, some forms of creativity and innovation initiatives require deep expertise and concerted effort best accomplished through highly specialized units. There are important competitive reasons why new product development teams function in secrecy and isolation. On the other hand, creative problem solving to prevent or minimize the impact of threats, surprises, and disasters should be everyone's forte. We have also noted how innovation is becoming more open-sourced, with many additional actors involved across and outside the organization.

The essential capabilities and specific skills for dealing with both the requisite variety and shared ownership for innovation require full attention to building High AR. Given the need for differentiated innovation scripts and broad-based engagement in resourceful activities, we offer development recommendations keyed to each of the four levels.

Developing Resourceful Individuals

Consistent with previous recommendations for developing other High AR qualities, the first challenge is for you to identify the individuals in the organization with the personal characteristics and job-related skill sets associated with resourcefulness: an entrepreneurial spirit, flexibility, and a creative mind. Those individuals in relevant key positions—such as new product development team leaders, directors of major projects, managers of critical alliances and partnerships, those in key linking or boundary roles, managers at the leading edges of functions frequently called on for rapid responses—all can be targeted for assessments first.

There are several assessment tools to help you do this, but we are great fans of solo and team-based simulations and evaluations of people in actual problem-solving situations. We like Outward Bound and other structured team-building experiences for observing individuals in a variety of situations that require creative problem solving and innovative responses.

Once identified, these individuals can be provided development opportunities and assignments that test and sharpen those attributes. Their development should be monitored over time and they should be strategically placed in key team positions and leading-edge roles. Individuals with characteristics that do not fit the organization's creativity/innovation profile, such as rigid thinking and preferences for well-defined and structured situations, should be kept out of situations and teams where creative problem solving is expected. Sounds obvious, of course, but we have simply encountered too many situations where it must have appeared less than obvious.

Individuals must also work hard to develop the other High AR qualities discussed in other chapters, because they are all intertwined. For example, we noted in Chapter Four how sustained high pressure and anxiety are so detrimental to wellness, particularly cognitive functioning. Paying attention to personal wellness in all its forms and developing appropriate knowledge and skills are essential for stimulating curiosity, sharpening creativeness, and fostering flexibility. Create situations and safe spaces where individuals can play with ideas cooperatively without pressure, minimize unscheduled meetings and meeting changes, and protect time-pressured creatives as best as possible (Amabile, 2007).

Developing Resourceful Teams

We think the basic innovation unit in most organizations is the team; thus individuals need to fine-tune their skills in group dynamics and team leadership. Ideally, designated resourceful employees as described previously should be rotated across different teams and projects so that personal relationship networks can develop. Wellness in a team context is also critical because a team can only be as successful as its least-well member.

In addition, creative problem-solving skills in teams need to be finely honed. We are talking about more than an occasional LEGO-block building exercise or two-day university seminar. The organization needs to experiment with all four innovation scripts to identify the variety of roles, responsibilities, and ways in which individuals and teams engage the core processes associated with each. This involves team-level knowledge building and skill building through exposure to a variety of teams inside and outside the organization. We see value in getting a team to observe how other teams function in a range of settings. Creative organizations like IDEO also run professionally delivered workshops for groups on how to approach creative problem solving and design effective solutions with given resource parameters.

Developing resourceful teams also means staffing them with the right people. Team members should be cross-trained not only to create pools of redundant and overlapping knowledge and skills, but to help anticipate each other's actions. Team composition and balance in terms of cognitive styles and expertise should be explicit and ongoing topics of discussion between HR and line management. HR should be prepared to deliver a strong team development and assessment program. Attention to group dynamics, including the dynamics of trust, power, and confidence in each other's abilities, is fundamental. Preserving membership stability once a team is formed becomes a clear goal.

Teams also have to be integrated into all key organization processes, particularly communications and decision making, and supported with the right resources in sufficient quantity. The quality of information resources and technologies, and the skills of team members in using them quickly and effectively, are decisive. The quality and quantity of information accessible to the team will determine the range of solutions developed. In the case of *Apollo 13*, the ground team actually had access to another capsule simulator in which to test ideas that the crew could use to get home safely.

Developing Resourceful Organizations

A feature of High AR Resourceful organizations worth noting is their ability to deploy and redeploy resources quickly. The goal is to enable teams to form, re-form, engage each other, and share resources on an as-needed basis. That goal runs contrary to the culture of many organizations where resource hoarding by business units and teams may still be the norm, especially in tough times. Replicating resources for each and every business unit and team is not the goal. What needs development is the capability for fast starts and rapid deployment and redeployment of sufficient resources to the place most needed at the time.

Think about how easily or how poorly this is accomplished in your own organization. In Google, for example, highly defined business units are avoided, and the specific project or product becomes the focus for allocating resources within the parameters of clear performance metrics. Managers talk about which opportunities need funding and much less about the funding of a business unit itself (Manyika, 2011). Money and people flow to opportunities, not organization boxes. There are design complications from such practices, as we noted in Chapter Six, but the point is that barriers and obstacles to resource flows—people, money, or equipment—must be minimized.

There are other ways to stimulate agility by removing barriers to creativity. One way is to literally think through the structural barriers to ideas moving and people interacting. We are not necessarily fans of open office environments, and the debate rages about how much privacy or sharing of space is appropriate, but strategically locating people in proximity to each other and making sure they are linked through sophisticated but friendly technologies are sound suggestions. Some barriers seem to be innately human. The flow of ideas through an organization's innovation circuitry is usually controlled by key gatekeepers, such as VPs for projects, chief engineers, and directors of R&D labs. It is essential that these gatekeepers governing idea movement are identified and either supported or replaced, depending on the strength of their contribution in the innovation value chain (Cross, Hargadon, Parise, & Thomas, 2007).

HR plays a critical role in supporting innovation as the Institute for Corporate Productivity (i4cp) has recognized. In 2011, i4cp published several reports and white papers on the role of HR in the innovation process (see www.i4cp.com); other organizations, including the Center for Creative Leadership (CCL), have made a similar case.

Making sure that the culture of an organization recognizes and rewards creativity and innovation is critical for generating Being Resourceful behaviors. Reward and incentive systems have received considerable attention in this regard, but we also include job designs as a key feature. As Robert Shapiro, NutraSweet's former CEO and later Monsanto CEO, once noted as a design guideline, "Big jobs make big people. Small jobs make small people" (McCann, 1990)—meaning that individuals' thinking and skills expand with the scope of their job. This can reach an extreme, as many people now feel after years of downsizing, but there is no question that broadly and openly defining job responsibilities creates greater degrees of freedom for entrepreneurial thinking and action, which can be rewarding and motivating when provided to the right people.

As we note in the next chapter, the organization must also promote the development of fully functioning formal and informal communication networks inside and outside the organization if information and ideas are to flow quickly and broadly. Networks should not be accidental creations and their composition and functionality need to be explicitly recognized and systematically developed if the speed and richness of decision making is to improve. Networks grow in unpredictable ways and degrade quickly if left unattended.

Finally, we have stressed the importance of developing capabilities and combining them in new ways as an aspect of an adaptive design mindset. Essentially we are asserting that through Being Resourceful, High AR organizations have developed the capability of executing all four types of innovation scripts described in this chapter. They are effective at routine tactical innovation and strategic corporate innovation, and can also engage in fast-cycle problem solving and improvisation when needed. We believe that competence in all four scripts will be increasingly tested in turbulent environments going forward. These organizations are not just ambidextrous—they are multidextrous.

Achieving this capability is not necessarily as formidable as it may sound. All of these scripts already occur in most organizations to some extent. What we advocate is the thoughtful, systematic development of the specific sets of competencies and skills associated with each script, combined with the judgment to deploy the appropriate one for the right situation.

These practices tap into both agility and resiliency. As we have discussed, creativity and innovation should be cultivated not just to take advantage of opportunities but also to prepare for problem situations requiring resiliency. Coming up with agile, creative ways of taking advantage of an opportunity is wonderful; so is coming up with resilient, creative ways of preventing an event from damaging business performance. Creativity and innovation are applied and valued in both kinds of situations. The kinds of questions you should be asking are: Are we as creative and innovative as we need to be in developing and implementing a global risk-management process? Have we prepared ourselves to have the first planes back in the air after a national crisis?

Developing Resourceful Ecosystems

We have no doubt that this level is receiving increasing attention. The resourcefulness of interdependent organizations and groups —whether they are linked tightly or loosely—is seen as both a competitive advantage and a source of great concern. The Great Recession was brought about by weakly restrained creativity and innovation in financial products and practices by some big players in the financial services industry. It was collaboratively produced because seemingly everyone benefited—until it unraveled.

A critical question in terms of Being Resourceful is whether those within the ecosystem have the collective resources and skills for dealing with the consequences of their behaviors. A second question is whether they have access to the additional resources needed if the answer to the first question is "no." These questions deal with ecosystem resiliency. Chapter Eight deals with both of these concerns in detail. As of this writing, however, we have to conclude that these questions remain unanswered for the Great Recession, more than three years after the precipitating events that set that train wreck in motion. Neither of us feels comfortable thinking about improvisation as the dominant innovation script now in use for managing the global financial system.

The flip side of resiliency at the ecosystem level is the agility of its organizations and groups in identifying and collectively taking advantage of opportunities presented to members. Global supply chains continue to evolve as world conditions change. Other kinds of value creation and innovation networks also operate across the globe, but we believe that this is the area where considerably more thinking and design will occur in the future. The "open source" software movement is a vibrant case in point. Needless to say, we advocate good strategic boundary management in such networks as they also pose considerable risk in terms of the loss of intellectual property and poorer, not better, performance due to disruptions.

Finally, although information and logistics technologies allow ever greater distributed collaboration and virtual work systems, we continue to see increasing clustering and colocation of organizations in the same industry within "creative communities" (Florida, 2005). A broad set of stakeholders in Central Florida, for example, has been involved in economic development along the "I-4 Corridor." It is inevitable that comparisons are made to Silicon Valley, the North Carolina Research Triangle, and other area technology clusters. It may be risky to build physical capacity and "hard" network infrastructure for creative and innovative behavior as the Internet disperses talented creatives around the globe. The skills and sustained investment of resources needed to build new innovation clusters are formidable. Still, Singapore and cities and regions in India, Brazil, and China appear to be mastering the challenge of building resourceful innovation clusters. As the Western economies languish, these BRIC nations are demonstrating tremendous agility and resiliency through their attention to ecosystem-level development of AR capabilities.

chapter
EIGHT

Engaged Networking

We struggled to name the fifth High AR capability in our framework. We looked at data, recalled conversations with company executives, and wrestled with a thesaurus to understand what we were observing. Some observations were straightforward. At an individual level, we noted in Chapter Four how individuals with well-developed relationships in their personal and professional lives are healthier; that is, they have greater social wellness. Building on this, research tends to support the premise that individuals with larger networks of friends and associates are happier and physically healthier.

At the next level, teams with well-developed internal relationships with other members perform better, make sense of situations more effectively, and take action more quickly. When they are embedded in an organization's networks and linked effectively within its structure, they also perform better because they have pathways into key resources, communications, and decision-making processes. Both individuals and teams gain meaning and reinforce their sense of alignment and purpose through their relationships. These observations are important, given the strong connections among wellness, purposefulness, and High AR.

Similarly, organizations perform more effectively when they are part of well-developed and integrated networks in their ecosystems. Through their interactions with stakeholders and other ecosystem players, they can create shared appreciations of situations and advocate positions that promote their common interests. Those shared appreciations become the basis for collaborative responses, which are more effective and efficient than going it alone. In turn, their collaborative actions help to create less turbulent, more defensible social space that essentially pushes turbulence further from their operating space. Other authors (Hart, 2010; Kanter, 1994, 2003) have noted how organizations can and do create "collaborative advantage" as well as competitive advantage by working together in alliances and associations toward common goals. These are all important features of AR, but simply calling this quality networking hardly does the concept justice.

Management researchers became interested in social networks in the 1970s, and imported concepts like centrality, tie strength, and degrees of separation from sociology and anthropology. We encountered one concept in a dusty corner of the management literature—"to reticulate," which means to create a net, as in a fishing net. In the academic literature, however, a *reticulist* is someone who weaves—that is, designs and manages—a network of connections in a social system such as an organization, community, or industry (B. Cohen, 1983; Gray, 1985).

What is the difference between "reticulating" and "networking"? The underlying concepts are quite similar, but Being Networked as a capability is concerned with the systematic creation and support of a structured network of valuable relationships that are actively managed and used to support both agile and resilient responses. There is an element of intentional design and use in reticulating not found in networking.

The lessons from Chapter Six regarding strategic boundary management are worth recalling. Here we want to draw out implications of Being Action-Oriented for an organization's networking activity. What were the outcomes for Lehman Brothers and Sandler O'Neill after each firm experienced devastating losses (financial in the former, human in the latter)? What made the larger organization *not* worth saving and the smaller one so valuable that it attracted dozens of volunteers, even some from competitors and clients, to help get it back on its feet (Freeman, Hirschhorn, & Maltz, 2004; Whitford, 2011)? Arguably, Lehman Brothers created its own crisis while Sandler O'Neill's was externally induced. However, we believe the answer lies in the quality of their relationships in their respective networks. Being Networked for High AR means that an organization is part of an agile and resilient network. In practice this means that an organization can mobilize others in the network not only to act for the benefit of the whole network, but also to assist one of its members when that member is overwhelmed by an event. Are others prepared and able to share resources in time of great need? For Lehman Brothers, the answer was no; for Sandler O'Neill, the answer was yes.

Chapter Six also posed questions about downside risk such as: Are some relationships simply so difficult to manage in terms of the time, attention, and resources devoted to them that you wonder why you have them? Are the risks associated with doing business with another firm so great, despite its attractive products or services, that you would be crazy to engage with them? It is worthwhile reflecting on these questions if you want to build this fifth capability.

We also inquired about upside opportunities in Chapter Six, following on from our discussion about learning in Chapter Five. We asked, Whom do you best learn from and how can you promote great creative chemistry within your network? If innovation and creativity are collective processes that happen in teams and even ecosystems, then your challenge is to seek out the very best possible complementary skills. That search process requires that you access preexisting networks or perhaps building one fresh. Your skills in some aspect of product design may be strong, for example, but how can you quickly add variety with complementary skills in your network? Creating a reliable way of outsourcing product design functions across a global network is daunting, but thanks to new collaborative technologies, your network may be regional, continental, or global. Remember: The world is flat (Friedman, 2005)! Entire books are written about these challenges, and what we can best provide here are some useful metrics associated with creating those relationships with AR in mind.

Consider the case of large software and Internet-based giants such as Microsoft, Yahoo, Amazon, and Google, as Bala Iyer, Chi-Hyon Lee, and N. Venkatraman did in their 2006 *California Management Review* article "Managing in a 'Small World Ecosystem': Lessons from the Software Industry." The companies they studied "are all connected in a complex and fast changing web of competition and cooperation" (p. 28). They form alliances that create or shift centers of influence within their sectors while supporting interoperability. For such networks to perform well, these authors offered several prescriptions, such as creating performance dashboards for the network calibrated with appropriate metrics, and mapping and managing the roles and responsibilities played by the various network actors.

In our discussion of strategic boundary management in Chapter Six we also advocated that managers consciously design and cultivate those relationships to maximize their quality at acceptable costs and risks but prevent *excessive* connectedness. In this chapter we provide several of the concepts and metrics for gauging the robustness of networks at all levels and for building your skills as a reticulist—an effective builder of networks.

Networks and Stakeholders

Networks in a business context are the topography on which business is conducted. Internal networks connect individuals and teams within an organization; they extend vertically (authority and formal communication networks), horizontally (peer-to-peer communication networks), and laterally (project team and special-interest networks). External networks connect an organization with its various stakeholders. Some external networks are directly relevant for furthering an organization's strategy and accomplishing its mission, such as a company's connections through its supply chain. Other external networks are indirectly relevant for goal accomplishment, such as a company's connections to local area charities through its philanthropic activities. From a social wellness perspective, those relationships can be very important, as we have noted.

All of these external organizations populate the ecosystem level we have discussed throughout this book. We use the term ecosystem broadly in this book, but Marco Iansiti and Roy Levien, in their 2004 *Harvard Business Review* article which popularized the term in a business context, note a distinctive aspect of a business ecosystem that we have not stressed up until now. For them, a business ecosystem is composed of a "keystone" or lead firm that establishes the platform and infrastructure for the other firms ("niche players") in the ecosystem. It isn't just a loose grouping or set of organizations, but one with a center or focus—a central node of a network. This way of understanding business ecosystems advances the concept of the "value constellation" first articulated by Richard Normann and Rafael Ramirez in 1993, also in the *Harvard Business Review.*

Interest groups and stakeholders populate the landscape of an ecosystem. Through interactions with specific stakeholders such as suppliers and regulators, a company routinely operates in multiple external networks attempting to further its strategy and accomplish its mission. Some networks transcend the direct goal-oriented interests of any organization; these are the issue-specific networks that last only as long as that issue has salience. An organization may, for example, become a stakeholder in an issue such as health care reform, local education funding, or climate change. Large and small organizations wield considerable power to instigate, advance, or retard such public issues (that is, issues shared by multiple stakeholders), through partnerships like the World Business Council for Sustainable Development (Marot, Selsky, Hart, & Reddy, 2005; Selsky & Parker, 2005).

Whether corporations should or should not participate in such issues is really not even debatable in a capitalist democracy that recognizes corporations as legitimate entities, but occasionally an issue has a very vocal advocate. In a full-page advertisement that raised eyebrows in mid-2011, Howard Schultz, CEO of Starbucks, began advocating to his fellow CEOs that businesses boycott corporate contributions to federal political campaigns until serious progress had been made on issues such as the U.S. budget deficit (2011, p. 8). Ecosystems energized by such key stakeholders can have a great impact on the prevailing tone and sentiment of people in a region or country.

The study and design of stakeholder relations in ecosystems is an art form in itself. Whether transitory and issue-specific or durable and institutionally mandated, ecosystems are major players that shape environmental dynamics. They can either buffer or exacerbate turbulence affecting your organization and therefore deserve your full attention and active management. There are specific aspects of these networks that are worth focusing on, and we want to touch on those before diving into network metrics.

Growth of the Global Supply Chain

First, global supply chains, value chains, or extended enterprises (Blanchard, 2010; Christopher, 2005; Friedman, 2005) are particular types of organized ecosystems. Their emergence is arguably one of the social innovations with the greatest impact on the conduct of business over the past thirty years. These include complex supply chain ecosystems built and maintained by keystone firms like Toyota Motors, Nike, and Walmart (A. Iyer, Seshadri, & Vasher, 2009). For us, global supply chains are the main game regarding networks. They have become the lifeblood of many organizations and must be given the attention and resources to sustain them in turbulent conditions because they pose such major risks to the global economy. Their impact is not truly appreciated until a supply chain breakdown in another part of the world is felt within days in a local and regional economy.

There are huge ecosystem-level AR issues associated with global supply chains, as we have noted in previous chapters. Those issues are largely due to problems associated with the membership rigidity and geographical concentration of some supply chains. Inflexibility is caused by the large capital investments necessary for some operations or the highly specialized skills of some members that are hard to duplicate. Large investments in fixed assets such as logistics centers are not readily abandoned, particularly if shared with supply chain partners. Nor can a supply chain partner's hard-to-replace skills and capabilities be quickly abandoned. Inflexibility may make them more susceptible to disruptions if the performance of one or more members is compromised. For example, the computer chip industry experienced disruptions during the SARS outbreak in Asia over a decade ago, the auto industry encountered weak links during the Japanese earthquake and tsunami, and disk drive makers found supply bottlenecks when heavy flooding occurred in Thailand in late 2011. Recently, the consequences of climate change have become a factor in global operations planning, and supply chain agility and resiliency are increasingly a concern (Sheffi, 2005). Companies such as Intel, Starbucks, and Walmart—keystone firms in their respective business ecosystems—are acutely aware of these issues.

Networking and Knowledge Management

Second, global supply chains only function through well-designed and supported knowledge management systems. A firm's information technologies are the foundation for communicating and sharing the information and knowledge needed to enable the firm to work effectively. We know, however, that there are both hard and soft systems for creating, building, sharing, and retaining useful information and converting it to advantage. A thoughtfully designed KM process will assure that relationships are supported across individuals and groups. The process is not just about collecting, moving, and retaining information.

Although a lot of knowledge within your organization and supply chain may be explicit, just as much, if not more, is implicit—contained within the minds of knowledge workers and embedded in the routines of groups and teams. Most organizations today are keenly aware of the importance of effectively designing and deploying information systems to collect, organize, and share tacit knowledge. Expert lists, key word–searchable archives of studies and reports, intranets, and other internal communications systems are widely in use.

Soft systems are therefore widely and deliberately used. For example, organizations as well as networks of organizations in the same ecosystem participate in communities of practice to build and share knowledge. Research on this phenomenon over the past two decades reveals that these knowledge-based communities can be physical or virtual and fluid in membership across time and organizational boundaries (Nonaka, 1991; Wenger, 1998). Such communities are common; we see them in industry trade associations and local chambers of commerce, and they extend to more specialized professional groups. When supported by a shared communications platform, these networks can nicely complement enterprise supply chain systems like SAP, boosting overall ecosystem agility. Large-scale Oracle- or SAP-based systems are being supported with different kinds of "soft" systems that add texture and color to raw data.

We think that you can benefit by fostering informal social networks to support formal systems. For example, we particularly like the way some organizations are starting to build networks early in the career tracks of high-potential individuals who will later become leaders across a globally dispersed company. Microsoft, for example, creates talent pools of younger high potentials whose members interact with each other in multiple structured ways over time. The relationships they create with each other early on become the basis for faster, more confident collaboration and coordinated decision making later as they spread out across the globe. This is an old, tried-and-true HR strategy used in many companies as well as the Catholic Church and cohort MBA programs. Companies like IBM and Shell Oil use it too, but they also constantly move employees around the world to build their world view and infuse them with the company culture in a global context. The newer tech companies do it for some of the same reasons, and understand very well the tremendous benefits of networking.

The Rise of Social Media

Finally, the newest exciting development in the global village during the past decade is the rise of technology-rich social media, and this has big implications for business networking (Gossieaux & Moran, 2011; Qualman, 2011). Given the huge success and exponential growth of social networking via the Internet, our argument for networking as an AR strategy may sound obvious and rather late in the game. Still, the evident power of social networks is worth acknowledging and exploiting. Just how powerful is social networking? As an example, the dozen or more matchmaking Web services such as Match.com or eHarmony.com claim credit for a significant percentage of U.S. marriages each year (Bialik, 2009). Facebook has over 750 million registered users, 50 percent of whom log in at least once a day, and is working through an initial public offering (IPO) as we write this book, while LinkedIn went public in 2011 with its own successful IPO and claims 120 million members in over 200 countries. How accurate these statistics may be is up for debate, but they are indicators of the importance and effectiveness of networking.

Despite their formidable scale, social media are still in their early development stages and fraught with abuses and risks, as some U.S. congressmen and political candidates in 2011 can attest. Social media environments are still essentially designed around individuals in their loose-knit groups of friends and associates.

Businesses, however, are catching on to social media to build market presence, relate to customers, and manage public perceptions. In some respects, organizations are interlopers into social-media communities and there is a healthy debate about the impact of businesses on the culture and climate of social media environments (Qualman, 2011). It is facile to advise companies not to get into that game unless they are prepared to devote the staff and resources that social media demand. Many companies now have no choice in an era when "tagging" or posting a malicious comment or image about a company or product on Facebook has become a popular pastime. It may take someone only a few minutes to post a negative item about a company, but that company can spend days trying to find and correct it. Francois Gossieaux and Ed Moran say it well by noting, "Ubiquitous connectivity to others (usually via some sort of wireless connection) creates far more opportunity for your customers, your potential customers, and your detractors to move from thinking about your company to saying or doing something about your company. Such connectivity also permits tsunamis of sudden sentiment about your company to rise incredibly fast" (Gossieaux & Moran, 2011, p. 16).

Going further, Gossieaux and Moran claim that savvy organizations "will not use social media as a new channel to reach and interact with customers; instead, they will realize that social media fundamentally changes the way you identify, develop, educate, and support those customers" (Gossieaux & Moran, 2011, p. 17). Organizations will need to become "hyper-social" to meet these challenges.

In terms of the topic of this chapter, the use of social media by business represents an arena where networking is focused outward. At a workgroup level, social media are also finding work-related uses in building and maintaining internal relationships across geographically dispersed teams. It is a fast, richly textured form of interaction that e-mail cannot match. Nice to know that Sanjay in Bangalore likes skin-diving; makes him more a person than an e-mail address. Our students remind us that "e-mail is for old people" and are forcing us to communicate with them via Facebook to make sure they read our messages—as they shamelessly text away in our classrooms. However, some public school districts around the United States are now limiting teachers' use of Facebook and Twitter for communicating with students for privacy reasons.

Other forms of group-based communications are taking hold for knowledge creation, sharing, and team collaboration. Choose your provider, but the overall industry trend, according to ABI Research and MSP News (ABI Research, 2011) is that managed telepresence and videoconferencing services will exceed $1.2 billion in annual revenue by 2016. And, of course, there are dozens of Web-conferencing platforms for the myriad webinars offered internally by companies and externally by hundreds of professional associations just within the United States. Given the time, cost, and inconvenience of air travel these days, this makes a lot of sense.

The rise of social media illustrates an important point about networking. Although many networks are highly formalized and stable, such as the global supply chains discussed earlier, others are transitory and issue or opportunity specific. Cross-sector partnerships focused on social causes may not actually operate like a formal network but more like specific project-based engagements (Selsky & Parker, 2005). They form, perform, and disperse, a process made much easier through social media. The power of such temporary and ad hoc networks, supported by social media such as Facebook and Twitter, was vividly illustrated in Tunisia and Egypt in the Arab Spring of 2011, as well as in a variety of new social movements springing up around the world.

Assessing the AR Value of Networks

As the amount and variety of information bombarding all of us accelerates and the demands on our time and attention keep rising, we risk becoming "hyperconnected," according to Terry Retter (2001). With the push toward greater agility and opening the organization to its environment, interdependencies with the environment proliferate. Businesses in global supply chains and value constellations are good examples.

When we add concerns about resiliency to the mix it is clear that organizations need to manage risk exposures more diligently and be willing to buffer external interdependencies by creating boundaries. That is the essence of our recommendations regarding strategic boundary management in Chapter Six. We know that high-performing individuals, teams, organizations, and their ecosystems are characterized by well-developed networks of valuable relationships that are actively managed to promote AR.

Given the many forms and ways of networking, how can you judge which ones best support High AR for your organization? This is a key strategic issue because "capturing cross-business synergies is at the heart of corporate strategy . . . yet synergies are notoriously challenging to capture," as Kathleen Eisenhardt and Charles Galunic (2000, p. 91) put it. So let's consider the criteria that a good reticulist needs to apply in capturing value in a network. Being Networked consists of maintaining network relationships that are valuable, pose acceptable costs and risks, and are highly reliable. We consider each criterion in the following sections.

Relationship Value

A valuable relationship is one that helps to generate new knowledge or test reality against what you perceive or believe to be the case in an ambiguous situation. Such a relationship is richly textured, meaning that it is easily accessible and interactive, providing multiple ways of connecting to others. Perhaps most importantly, those involved in the relationship have substantial adaptive capacity and access to sufficient resources if called upon. General Motors, Chrysler, AIG, and a number of major U.S. banks were glad to have relationships of value when the economy began falling apart and bailouts were needed in 2008–2009. This may sound crassly utilitarian, and it is; organizations need to use networking strategically—and ethically.

Clearly, new knowledge has use, and knowledge that reduces ambiguity and helps confirm or disconfirm something sensed has great value. It's important for you to cultivate smart friends who are well connected to what is going on. Scott McNealy, former CEO of Sun Microsystems, used to talk about seeking out "lighthouse" customers—the leading-edge, creative ones—because he could learn the most from them. If an organization's KM process is able to flag crucial knowledge gaps or challenges, then finding experts in the network that can fill those gaps is invaluable.

Rich texture refers both to the nature of the content and the medium in which it is exchanged. A relationship that is merely exchanges of information or data is cold. In a richly textured relationship the data or information comes with emotional meaning, vibrancy, and contextual implications communicated through open exchanges and inquiry. That may partially explain the power of social media like Facebook.

Accessibility means that a relationship is flexible and adaptive and can be accessed many times and in different ways. Relationships in a turbulent environment have to be more than just proscribed, contractual obligations. When events move quickly, everyone involved or affected must be accessible and able to communicate and engage with each other as demanded by the situation. Interacting through multiple channels and forms, such as colocating or near-shoring as opposed to off-shoring, allows for real-time interaction.

Not all relationships have to have all of the above attributes, but we believe all the attributes must exist somewhere in the set of relationships if the network is to be effective in supporting the organizations within it.

Acceptable Costs and Risks

In Chapter Six we stressed that managers should use the criteria of costs and risks to assess their relationships in terms of strategic boundary management. The key qualifier is acceptable costs and risks. You may have a valuable relationship that also carries high maintenance costs, such as plants and logistics centers near a key customer's location. You accept those costs because of the value delivered by the relationship. It is a cost/benefit trade-off made by companies every day.

Now introduce the concept of risk into the trade-off calculus. If a supplier creates unacceptable risks in its relationship with a buyer firm, despite its high value and acceptable costs, then the buyer firm must decide whether that relationship should be maintained. An example is the Chinese subcontractor, Foxconn, that threatened Apple's reputation with its poor work practices, described in Chapter Four. Apple reacted and made Foxconn improve its work practices after studying how Nike had faced similar concerns a decade earlier. Apple is making additional efforts to gauge that risk over time with its monitoring and certification system. Global risk management is a major profitable practice area for all the large accounting firms. Our concern is that most organizations are still not very adept at introducing risk estimates into the value/cost calculations of their relationships. To get better at it you will need to develop your risk-management thinking—and fast (Pearson & Mitroff, 1993; Perrow, 2007; Weick & Sutcliffe, 2007).

Depending on their industry and markets, all organizations must cope with different kinds of risk—reputation, supply-chain, currency, technology, competitive leapfrogging, ecological, and so on. A thorough review of these is not within the scope of this book, but your organization is likely to face more intense risks and more kinds of risks in a turbulent environment. In addition to these risks encountered in the present, a turbulent environment also amplifies future risk. It becomes less likely that historical trajectories of important variables—from currency exchange rates to weather patterns—will continue relatively undisturbed into the volatile future. Trying to take into account future risk and the variety of present risks in the networking calculus becomes a formidable task indeed. This is especially true for what Karl Weick and Kathleen Sutcliffe (2007) call "high reliability organizations" such as nuclear power plants, hospitals, and utilities, as compared with most other organizations that are designed for high efficiency.

Stress-Testing Relationships

Trying to immediately mobilize a network to seize a great opportunity or manage the aftermath of major shock is not the time to test the reliability of the relationships with others you must count on to deal with the situation. High AR Networked organizations stress-test their critical relationships periodically to see how they react under extreme conditions. This is not the same as contingency planning which, unfortunately, never fares well in environments characterized by unique new conditions and novel events that blindside you.

The new One World Trade Center rising from the collapsed World Trade Center towers site will use high-rise design concepts that overcome the design flaws masked in the previous buildings until the totally unexpected occurred (Tischler, 2011). As another example, when General Electric designed and built the Fukushima nuclear facilities in Japan, their design specifications exceeded the safety standards set for hundred-year earthquakes in that region; however, the March 2011 earthquake and tsunami exceeded those standards. As we noted in the last chapter, the creative problem solving and improvisation demonstrated by so many individuals under the extreme conditions that followed in those reactors were extraordinary—and should never have been necessary. But they often become necessary in extremely disruptive, turbulent environments.

Such crisis situations are why Being Resourceful is so important to High AR organizations, as described in Chapter Seven. We have also strongly advocated scenario planning, search conferences, and simulations for encouraging sensemaking. However, these techniques can also be useful for testing the value and acceptability of costs and risks in relationships among those involved. Such exercises should be collaborative processes that engage a wide diversity of network members to broaden the range of perspectives. As such exercises unfold, it becomes apparent that organizations have different abilities for working well together under extreme conditions. We believe that those positive capabilities usually become known over time to others in a network, and everyone begins seeking relationships with those who have reputations for reliability and collaborative expertise.

It is also not enough just to offer up best, most likely, and worst-case scenarios in these stress tests. We are calling for really worst-case scenarios in which network members are severely stressed, even past the point of failure where the network collapses. These are essential opportunities for you to learn about your partners.

Such was nearly the case facing the Federal Reserve and U.S. Treasury, along with other central banks and global financial institutions, in the Great Recession. Even as we write this book, the global financial system continues to flirt with disaster. Charles Perrow's 2007 book *The Next Catastrophe: Reducing Our Vulnerabilities to Natural, Industrial, and Terrorist Disasters,* and Thomas Homer-Dixon's 2006 book *The Upside of Down: Catastrophe, Creativity, and the Renewal of Civilization,* are two of a growing number of books that illustrate how these and other institutional network collapses might unfold.

Once stress tested, it is time for interventions to do several things: improve those relationships worth preserving, create risk-management strategies for others, learn which relationships should be eliminated, and begin thinking about which new ones are now needed to fill gaps.

Recommendations for Being Networked

Being High AR Networked begins with recognition and systematic mapping of the key interpersonal and team networks that operate in your organization, as well as the ecosystem-level networks of which your organization is a part. Several software programs are available for this terrain mapping to create visual images that identify key knowledge exchange nodes and the directionality of those flows.

It is also essential to trace and map the critical second-, third-, and fourth- order relationships in the network. It may well not be your closest network partner that causes problems, but rather *its* partners that are only indirectly interdependent with you. For example, analysis of the Great Recession revealed that it was the underlying quality of the subprime home mortgage loans that had been originated, bundled, rebundled, and sold to successive financial institutions that unraveled the securitized-debt markets. More recently, the Japanese earthquake and tsunami revealed that the third-order sub-suppliers to the second-order primary parts suppliers in Japan were smaller and had limited resiliency. Those small sub-suppliers became a serious constraint in how quickly the supply chains with U.S. auto producers could be reactivated. It may be necessary to involve a great many other network members to get a full picture of the operative network.

Network maps are momentary snapshots that can help you visualize your place in a larger system of relationships. Armed with the information from a network map, a model based on key criteria can then help you make decisions about the relationships portrayed. In Figure 8.1 we offer such a model based on the two "input" criteria for relationships presented in this chapter, value and costs/risks. As we have noted, value is multidimensional; it is

Figure 8.1. Assessing Network Relationships

	Low Cost/Risk	High Cost/Risk
Low Value	Eliminate as possible or find ways to add value.	Eliminate at once or create ways to reduce costs and risks, or add value to justify cost and risk.
High Value	Beneficial and needs to be nurtured and preserved.	Requires aggressive monitoring and active management, with search for ways to manage risks.

not just an economic measure. Costs and risks include the time, attention, and effort invested, not to mention the financial investments made to manage that relationship. Though quantitative assessments may be possible, qualitative judgments by a knowledgeable cross-disciplinary team are a fine starting point. Figure 8.1 summarizes the general prescriptions that come from posing high-low characterizations of value and cost/risk against each other. The content of the cells are our prescriptions for identifying and sustaining highly reliable and flexible relationships in each of the four types of relationships.

For Low Value/Low Cost and Risk relationships, the general prescription is either to eliminate them because they add little value, or to find ways to add value to them. In addition, pruning the total number of low value interdependencies in the network may be worthwhile in a highly turbulent environment, just to reduce the volume of contact points for contagion.

For Low Value/High Cost and Risk relationships, the prescription is simple: eliminate them. Determine if they can be replaced with ones that pose less costs and risks.

For High Value/Low Cost and Risk relationships, the prescription is also simple: preserve and build on them. In addition, try to understand the characteristics of those relationships to see if they can be replicated in other networks as these qualities are so beneficial.

Finally, and most challenging, are the High Value/High Cost and Risk relationships. These demand aggressive monitoring and active management. The danger lies in cutting the investment of time and attention devoted to such relationships by overlooking the risks inherent in them. We believe that is the wrong choice. It is more appropriate to explore how the potential costs and downside risks can be mitigated and managed. Reinsurance and hedging are, of course, heavily used to minimize financial risks.

A 2×2 matrix may appear rather simplistic for assessing a complex tangle of network relationships, but our point is that a systematic process should be undertaken to gauge the health of your major networks. We recommend an assessment annually, preferably tied to the strategic planning process.

Our second major recommendation is that you build your networking competencies and skills. These include competencies and skills for creating and sustaining alliances and joint ventures, as well as multi-organizational and serially linked networks like supply chains and issue-specific coalitions. Organizations have become particularly adept at building supply chains and outsourcing networks, but the agility and resiliency of many of these are now being questioned for a multitude of reasons: illusory cost savings, loss of intellectual property, and environmental disruptions. Networks can create substantial "collaborative advantage" when functioning well. We advocate development of effective networking competencies and skills to realize the full advantage of networks. Our research has unequivocally confirmed the importance of systematic networking as a critical High AR capability.

chapter
NINE

Bringing It All Together

We have taken you from a molecular brain chemical level to global innovation clusters in our attempt to explain how individuals, teams, organizations, and their ecosystems can understand turbulence and begin building the capabilities needed to master it. There is no need to be continually victimized by rapid and disruptive change, and high-performing organizations have recognized the competitive advantage created by building the five capabilities that we have named. We have discovered these capabilities through intensive global research and through our own conversations and work with a great variety of professionals and organizations. We have provided both a lens and framework for viewing how all of the development activities that may be taking place within an organization should reinforce and support each other.

Given the varied conceptual territory we have traveled, it is worthwhile to briefly revisit the previous chapters to summarize for you the key ideas and lessons offered. We then provide a useful illustration of the 4 × 5 matrix presented in Chapter Three, courtesy of Professor David Graham Hyatt of the Sam M. Walton College of Business at the University of Arkansas. He has worked with executives in Walmart on studies of their supply chain and sustainability practices, many being industry breakthroughs. David volunteered to examine our concepts from the point of view of what he has observed at Walmart. He found the framework helpful in relating their initiatives to other AR capabilities. Finally, at the end of this chapter we dwell on an important question: Who owns AR development in an organization?

Core Concepts and Lessons

Revisiting the chapters is necessary because of the sheer amount of highly varied topics and the levels at which we covered them. Each one is the subject for more intensive reading and reflection, using the extensive set of references throughout the book.

Lessons from Chapters One and Two

Chapters One and Two laid out the basic challenges facing organizations as the pace of change, which is challenging but manageable, becomes increasingly punctuated by disruptive change. It is the combination of rapid and disruptive change that is more sharply delineating the performance winners and losers competing to see who adapts. We noted how the nature of change itself is changing, moving from episodic to continuous to now disruptive forms. Unfortunately, the prevailing skills, competencies, and capabilities have simply been inadequate to meet the magnitude of the challenges now being encountered with this latest evolution of organization environments.

This is occurring at the individual level as overstressed and overwhelmed employees feel turbulence not only in their work, but also in their families, communities, and the larger world. Teams are increasingly challenged with membership turnover and work overloads. Moreover, organizations are dealing with more exogenous shocks and surprises in a variety of forms, many natural disasters, and many institutional crises, some self-inflicted. The example cited of a small business in Omaha having trouble extending a bank credit line due to the failure of the Greek government to deal with its mismanaged economy is not an exaggeration. Financial market volatility has become both extraordinary and commonplace, much of it driven by events outside national borders.

The ecosystems in which an organization operates might provide less disturbed, more defensible space if its members collaborate, share information and resources, and fully support each other. But entire ecosystems are also being compromised by great demographic and economic forces, coupled with literally earth-shattering natural disasters. The institutional protocols that have governed interactions among members of ecosystems have traditionally been weak, but they are proving even more inadequate under the strains of today's disruptive world. Whether Asian earthquakes, European government paralysis, or improbable "black swans," the sheer number of such events creates a cascading effect. Undermanaged ecosystems are exacerbating turbulence, not dampening it. It really is an unhappy situation for anyone not adept at running a fast race over bumpy terrain.

Our initial AMA/HRI (i4cp) research and subsequent analyses, however, recognized that turbulence is being experienced unevenly. We found that mastering, not just managing, turbulence is not only possible but strongly correlated with higher performance, measured in terms of competitiveness and profitability. It was the adaptive capacities of individuals, teams, organizations, and their ecosystems that made the difference. The empirical link to performance has not been well made in the management literature, so the search began to identify those specific factors that do make a difference.

Lessons from Chapter Three

Chapter Three made the case for agility and resiliency as two critical dimensions of adaptive capacity. Moreover, two major lessons came from this chapter. First, agility or resiliency alone is not adequate for dealing with turbulence. Agility alone can create excessive openness to the environment as boundaries are destroyed and undermanaged interdependencies proliferate. Resiliency alone may help stave off or lessen the full impact of negative environmental events, but an organization may not be able to quickly take advantage of the opportunities present in those same environments. You have to have *both* agility and resiliency—they are highly correlated but distinctly different dimensions of adaptive capacity. It's about High AR.

The second lesson is that focusing on agility and resiliency just at an organization level is unlikely to work. It has to happen simultaneously at the levels of individuals, teams, and ecosystem— "down, around, and up," as we termed it. Weak individuals lead to weak teams, weak teams to weak organizations, and weak member organizations cannot effectively support ecosystem-level collaborative initiatives. We have tried to demonstrate that the true management challenge lies in dynamically balancing development of both agility and resiliency at all four levels. That is the pitch, but how do you do it?

Lessons from Chapter Four

Chapter Four began to unpack the answer by exploring the foundational capability—*purpose* expressed as a strong core identity, manifested through clear and aligned values and beliefs, and supported by physical, psychological, and social wellness. In many respects, purposeful individuals are the essential building block for agility and resiliency. Lapses and underdeveloped skills and competencies at the individual level can undermine teams, and weakened teams can then undermine organization-level initiatives. We made the point that teams are the primary means for accomplishing work in organizations, so their failure due to weakened individual members has profound implications for organization performance.

Chapter Four made clear linkages from the cognitive to the behavioral manifestations of excessive turbulence. Turbulence exacts a heavy toll on purpose and wellness—dysfunctional behaviors, stress, overload—and that's what erodes AR, causing slower starts, sluggish avoidance of shocks, and inadequate responses at all levels.

This chapter also noted how purposeful thought and behavior at organization and ecosystem levels can be expressed well. Organizations must be clear about their purpose and the purpose expressed in their vision must have legitimacy to be viable. It is the organization's stakeholders that grant it legitimacy— the perception of sufficient value that it is worth preserving. The organization cannot confer legitimacy upon itself; that is an illusion. There just aren't that many organizations "too big to fail." Even when they don't fail, their intentions are suspect and their actions regulated.

Finally, we made a strong case for promoting wellness at the organization and ecosystem levels. Targeted wellness interventions make economic and AR sense. The ROI on wellness initiatives is established, although AR payoffs are harder to calculate. What value would you attach to an intellectually alert and fully engaged CEO and senior leadership team in your organization in the midst of a prolonged economic recession? Millions of dollars? Perhaps a billion dollars? Not out of question, really, if you consider the costs of a botched acquisition or delayed new product introduction. How would you go about calculating that value?

At an ecosystem level, would you trade a "demographically challenged" workforce in your industry in North America or Europe for a younger, energized workforce in China? Many companies are doing precisely that. However, if you are a U.S. defense contractor or place-bound company, that option may not be so readily available, and collaborative wellness initiatives within your set of competitors and suppliers may be the better bet. We noted, for example, that "Blue Zone" health improvement interventions are taking place at the community level around the world, including at the state level in the United States.

Lessons from Chapter Five

This chapter posed the basic question: How do you know what you know? This is a tough question to answer in a turbulent environment because turbulence erodes awareness. Most organizations are not nearly as mindful as necessary about how they learn and how they manage their knowledge. The chapter was not about tools and techniques for political risk assessment or methodologies for effective scanning. It focused on the mindsets and underlying processes that create sense from the swirling, competing ideas, events, and trends at various stages of development and decay. Two of the most central processes are organizational learning (OL) and knowledge management (KM), both critically concerned with how data transforms into information and then into actionable knowledge.

OL focuses on how mental maps and causal models of what is going on are created. At an organization or ecosystem level, the systematic use of alternative scenarios of the future by Shell Oil and TECO Energy provide nice illustrations of how OL can be managed collaboratively. We strongly advocated formal KM processes that focused on key knowledge challenges or gaps and tight integration into organization strategic thinking and action. However, the primary focus of the chapter is on the five S's—

Scanning, Sensemaking, Shaping, Sharing, and Storing—and how they should function as integrated elements of the Being Aware capability.

A basic premise of Chapter Five is that Being Aware should be a collaborative building process, whether among individuals at a team level or a group of organizations collaborating around a specific shared issue. We strongly advocated practicing responses to shared opportunities and issues with others.

Lessons from Chapter Six

Whenever we have discussions with others about agility and resiliency, it is assumed that we are always concerned about taking action, either proactively or reactively. What you should have learned from the previous chapters and the following ones is that actions alone can be ineffectual and damaging. Blindly acting without being firmly grounded in a sense of purpose and without effective sensemaking creates the potential for error precisely when there may be no time or margin for it.

Being Action-Oriented for High AR means being open to change and developing unique competencies for identifying, building, and bundling capabilities to meet the requirements of a given situation. This is the adaptive design mindset we advocated. Acting confidently and effectively also means focusing and managing cultures and linking strategies to them, building an aggressive goal orientation and proactive posture, and strategically managing boundaries for advantage and risk management.

Strategic boundary management (SBM) has an edgy aspect to it. We noted that it may feel like social triage, but also argued that organizations already do it all the time. We are just advocating doing it thoughtfully and systematically using clear criteria and practices associated with each of the three main strategies —boundary formation, defense, and destruction. The criteria should recognize the comparative value, costs, and risks associated with a specific relationship.

Lessons from Chapter Seven

It isn't enough simply to act; one must act creatively and innovatively to take advantage of a situation or minimize its impact. Being Resourceful means being able to use a variety of response repertoires or innovation scripts in creative ways depending on the magnitude of potential impact and the speed of response required. In Chapter Seven we explored four different innovation scripts—routine incremental, strategic corporate, improvisational, and fast-track team-based—along with their merits and limitations.

Highly resourceful organizations are also skilled at quickly deploying and redeploying resources where they are needed, and being creative in the use of what resources they do have. We referred to the concept of *bricolage* to describe this talent. Our basic admonition is that you have to match the variety posed by your turbulent environment with equally varied responses; there should not be just "one best way" for being creative and innovative. In a world of limitations and constraints, learning how to use your resources creatively and innovatively becomes a wonderful capability that separates high and low performers.

Lessons from Chapter Eight

Being Networked means being a "reticulist"—an active designer and manager of networks in order to create relationships that will be essential in responding quickly to opportunities, minimizing the negative impact of events, even saving you if things really get out of hand. We talked about having great allies, knowing them well, and developing roles and routines for activating your networks. We noted that organizations that have extensive global supply chains or that operate in innovation networks or clusters are now working even harder to make sure those networks function effectively. The recent Japanese earthquake and tsunami, just like the SARS outbreak a decade earlier, demonstrated the costs and risks associated with openness to the environment, our theme back in Chapter One.

We also examined the role of social media. We stated our belief that social technologies are where a great deal of the exciting future work will continue to occur regarding the development and strategic use of networks. Our admonition is to get really good at developing and using those networks and social technologies for managing challenges and opportunities. Our focus finally turned to the management of network relationships by stress-testing them and generally applying SBM practices to them.

Walmart: An Application of the Framework

Walmart is the largest retailer in the world, with FY2011 global net sales of $419 billion and operating income of $25.5 billion, for an operating profit margin of 6.1 percent. This gargantuan company is the largest private-sector employer in the United States, with approximately 1.5 million "associates," and with stores in 28 countries and over 2 million employees worldwide. Walmart has transformed the face of retailing not only in North America but around the world, and has been highly praised and roundly criticized for its efforts. Its aggressive low-cost business strategy, human-resource practices, relations with stakeholders, and extensive philanthropy program have attracted the attention of business scholars, resulting in several Harvard Business School cases and numerous other articles.

One of us participated in a three-hour workshop on cross-sector partnerships in 2009 at which managers from Walmart's sustainability-strategy office and from the Environmental Defense Fund (EDF) discussed a partnership they had forged the previous year. The workshop was organized by Dr. David Graham Hyatt of the Sam M. Walton College of Business at the University of Arkansas. In later conversations during the writing of this book, David offered to work with our five capabilities to make sense of what Walmart was doing and to assess whether their actions supported his cursory observations about their agility and resiliency. His commentary, backed up by multiple tables not presented here, is included in Exhibit 9.1.

Exhibit 9.1. High AR and Sustainability: Walmart's Sustainability Strategy

In October 2005, Lee Scott, then Walmart CEO, announced a dramatic turn in company strategy—it would drive change and innovation in the company using a lens of sustainability.* Over the next six years the company leveraged preexisting High AR and developed new capabilities. But the five preceding years were sufficiently rocky in terms of stakeholder pressure and consumer concerns that basic assumptions about the company were challenged. However, a strong sense of purpose endured and was perhaps even strengthened with the sustainability message. An ethos of "saving people money so they can live better," attributed to founder Sam Walton, dominates company action, embedded as it is in low-cost strategy. In his 2005 speech, Scott acknowledged the turnaround in perceptions of the company due to their extraordinary and publicly appreciated response to hurricane Katrina, asking: "What would it take for

*Contributed by David Graham Hyatt. This narrative is based on company interviews taken during 2011 and on public sources.

Walmart to be that company, at our best, all the time?" Current CEO Mike Duke continues this messaging, noting that "[sustainability is] the right thing to do ... [and] is really just a part of who we have become."

Walmart has long been criticized for being insular, and sustainability revealed a new dimension of awareness. The company opened its doors to critics, and as Lee Scott said, "We didn't send a delegation or committee to meet with our critics. I met with them, so did [other execs]. . . . Mostly we listened. And asked questions." The company now routinely hosts meetings with NGOs such as the Environmental Defense Fund, World Wildlife Fund, and the Clinton Global Initiative, many of which have been influential in sustainability initiatives. The company also leveraged an existing practice in the business known as "eat what you cook." One manager reported the transformative effects: "We did buyer trainings where we'd pull the buyers to wastewater treatment plants, and the landfill, and to different farms, all to see what it was like to eat what they cook. We felt like they were so powerful to go to. . . . And it was out of a trip to a melting glacier that I understood that, if I can go after energy as a proxy for cost, I can get into a system much more deeply." These stories, as well as sustainability achievements, are shared widely in the company.

As suggested by the previous quote, awareness and action coevolve. Even before its sustainability thrust, Walmart had a very action-oriented culture—they consider themselves "doers." Indeed, continuing

(Continued)

the narrative of the manager above, he illustrated how the sustainability mindset informs action: "you see the [product] as a piece of the system in which it lives," not just as a function of net revenue. He went on to describe a complete transformational redesign of the product, producing multiple sustainability and cost benefits from production casting to consumer use. From resourcefulness and networking perspectives, these kinds of innovations are enabled by staged processes—experiment, pilot, and implement—supported by formal sustainability project networks (for example, energy, textiles, electronics) that include diverse constituents from both inside and outside the company.

One director illustrated an approach in the energy context for bringing new technologies up to scale by leveraging network resources: "To be an advocate of sustainability by default means you can't stay in a silo. Walmart is unique in that its global scale, often, is large enough to affect the cost curve, but not to the degree you can if you engage government and industry [e.g., Target]. . . . The energy piece really is a common denominator for everybody's operation."

In July 2009, new CEO Mike Duke announced an initiative aimed at achieving product sustainability. To be legitimate and effective, the outcomes of this initiative would have to be created collaboratively, requiring a "consortium of universities that will collaborate with suppliers, retailers, NGOs and government to develop a global database of information on the lifecycle of products . . . from raw materials to disposal." Walmart subsequently provided a lead gift that was to establish The Sustainability Consortium. Wide boundary conditions were established in this initiative in order to fully engage and take advantage of the embedded network resources, a network it set about forming.

In the early 2000s Walmart's leaders were sensing a major shift in the larger environment around issues of environmental responsibility and sustainability. Though they may not have known the precise dimensions or form of these issues, they knew that the company could play a significant role in responding to it. Over a period of many months managers in the strategic planning office as well as cross-functional teams and leaders engaged in additional inquiry, conversations with environmental stakeholders, and corporate sensemaking, and this helped to shape the issues in ways the company could respond.

From David's commentary we are more convinced than ever before that Being Purposeful—acting purposefully—is the foundation AR capability. In his write-up he talks about the powerful images of the new vision that were created when key managers were taken on field trips to farms, landfills, and glaciers that were directly relevant to their work on the new initiative. These images drove the vision home. Similarly, in a very forward-leaning, action-oriented company, the linking of new knowledge and perspectives about sustainability provided new mental models to redirect multiple streams of action around sustainability. The result has been numerous innovative energy initiatives and new ways of working, illustrating the integral linkages between awareness, action orientation, and resourcefulness. The driving issue of sustainability is also inherently broad and requires an equally broad definition of boundaries and active collaboration with multiple parties in the larger ecosystem. Walmart is a strong keystone firm in its business ecosystem, and its global clout has given it a dominant role in shaping how its vendors could align themselves with its own vision while also leading to significant environmental performance improvements in the vendors' own organizations around the world.

David's commentary also demonstrates that our framework can be used to foster specific themes, such as sustainability, leadership, or ethics. The lessons of High AR need not be confined to an organization's overall business strategy.

Leading AR Development

When you have such an encompassing set of concepts like those presented in this book, the inevitable and critical question is: Who owns AR development? AR is much like organization designing, which involves nearly all aspects of the organization and every functional area. The chief human resource officer (CHRO) may have some pieces of the puzzle while the COO, CIO, and CEO have others. Organization designing is a contact team sport; it requires active engagement of many key actors in a team environment to do responsibly. The same is true for building AR. Nonetheless, the different individuals and their staffs have sets of responsibilities for which they must claim leadership.

CEO Responsibilities

As David Hyatt's description of Walmart's Lee Scott illustrates, the CEO has major responsibilities for assuring that the organization's sense of purpose—its core identity manifested through meaningful values and beliefs—is clearly articulated and expressed in actions and behaviors. Values and beliefs must be experienced personally, within the leadership team, and throughout the organization and into its ecosystem. Visiting a melting glacier is a particularly vivid way to make a point about improving energy use in a big-box store. Also consider the other values and beliefs expressed in earlier chapters, such as those encouraging entre-preneurial initiative and innovative thinking in Chapter Six, and ask how an organization's vision and mission can reinforce those. John Hogan of Broadridge Financial Solutions used stone masons building a cathedral to communicate about vision and purpose. Southwest Airlines has put its mission into sustainable operation perhaps more effectively than any other organization we know.

A critical CEO responsibility is to ensure personal and lead-ership team member wellness. The ship has to have seaworthy leadership in turbulent seas. A corny comparison? Sure, but losing key executives at critical moments can have serious con-sequences. As we note in Chapter Four, many executives are getting the message but many others still have not. The team needs to be tested under duress and offered honest critiques about their individual and collective performance in handling tough challenges.

It also requires creating a sincere learning culture where norms and assumptions that shape the prevailing mental models and mindsets of key people can be challenged for their fit with the actual conditions. The CEO is the leading proponent for building an organizational learning culture to support the devel-opment of viable knowledge management systems and processes. This may mean making modest investments, for example, in scan-ning systems and staff, or utilizing external consulting and advisory services at a time when every expense is scrutinized. Otherwise, the alternative choice is to fly blind just as the level of turbulence escalates.

Finally, the CEO is responsible for making sure that the orga-nization is as resourceful as possible. This means ensuring that multiple creativity and innovation scripts are cherished, prac-ticed, and continuously refined. Those kinds of investments are definitely not modest, but cutting R&D and losing innovative capabilities may mean emptying the product pipeline and being forced into a merger or acquisition as the only growth alternative. Innovate or die, the saying goes.

CIO Responsibilities

The chief information officer (CIO) has significant responsibilities for ensuring the creation and support of information technologies, tools, and systems. Information generation, assessment, and delivery as actionable knowledge in accessible ways when and where needed is one of the most critical responsibilities in fostering High AR. The CIO also needs to work with other executives in designing and delivering AR performance metrics data which helps ensure high performance and horizontal and vertical alignment.

These responsibilities are all elements associated with building a robust knowledge management platform and system. There is ongoing debate about how the design of KM processes are influenced when the IT folks take it over, but the reality is that a KM platform has to be capable of incorporating the information and knowledge needs of *all* your employees, even if there are tens of thousands of them scattered around the world. The platform has to be implemented in ways that make it valuable and accessible to be used, thus it must be designed with its users in mind.

COO Responsibilities

The chief operating officer (COO) or top executive responsible for manufacturing and supply chain management is also actively involved in AR development. We have emphasized how important it is to stress-test the flexibility and resiliency of the value constellations and chains in which the organization participates. Protecting those relationships is a critical responsibility and this is where a lot of hard thinking and tough decisions need to occur. It is in this area of responsibility that strategic boundary management is practiced with vigor as vendors are pruned, relationships with others strengthened through investments, and some relationships ended and operations either returned to the home nation or consolidated near shore.

CHRO Responsibilities

The chief human resource officer (CHRO) has become an increasingly important focus for leadership at the strategic change level (Wright, Pace, Boudreau, & Sartain, 2011). Although many senior HR executives may not feel prepared for such business leadership responsibilities, many others are ready and participate fully. So much of what this book has explored centers on the adaptive capacities of individuals and teams. For these reasons, we give the CHRO primary AR leadership responsibility.

This position and the HR professionals who support it play central roles in designing or choosing appropriate AR diagnostic tools for assessing the capabilities and skills of individuals and teams in key positions, and for selecting new employees. In addition, HR usually owns the development and implementation of wellness programs. Other key support processes such as reward and incentive systems need to be evaluated and designed to support High AR behaviors in all the dimensions described in this book. This includes designing, in collaboration with the CEO, the rollout and acceptance of the organization's vision through sophisticated communications strategies and interventions to build organization–employee alignment and engagement.

One of the most critical functions of this leadership responsibility is targeting and assessing the agility and resiliency of key teams, particularly the top managers running major business units and in the C-suite leadership team. Recall the story in Chapter Four about the M&A process that temporarily derailed because of poor M&A team work conditions and the untimely heart attack of one member. The well-being of these leadership teams is critically important during periods of prolonged stress that impair physical, psychological, and social wellness. Development plans need to be created for individuals within those teams and for entire teams to make sure they are functioning at high levels. Ensuring that this is done becomes even more important in organizations where leadership turnover has occurred and new team members enlisted.

Finally, the CHRO and supporting professionals have important educational responsibilities for developing the specific bodies of knowledge, competencies, and skills needed for effective performance in each of the AR capability domains. This alone is a formidable, long-term undertaking that requires extensive training and development work across individuals and teams. The lists are long and for individuals include such learning objectives as:

- Developing abilities for self-reflection and self-mastery
- Empowering employees to manage their own wellness
- Contributing to team outcomes with solid problem-solving, decision-making, and communications skills
- Building systems thinking and sensemaking abilities about world events—knowing what is going on and how to think rationally about choices and consequences
- Enhancing creative problem solving in team contexts, often under pressure
- Managing relationships astutely in personal and professional networks
- Participating effectively in damage control teams in high-consequence situations

The list for teams is just as long and has many of the same objectives. Teams need to be able to reflect upon and assess their performance under different conditions and overcome any weaknesses discovered. There is a long and extensive literature about the characteristics of effective work teams and that knowledge needs to be put to use in building team-level capacities.

Organizations also need to acquire superior capabilities in the areas discussed. In Chapter Four we talked about the importance of assessing and assuring alignment of values and beliefs across levels, for example, and this work requires a great deal of honesty and candor to do well. Alignment work does not come easy for many senior executives, and the CHRO may need to play a coaching role with them to make sure it is done well. Similarly, in Chapter Six we talked about an adaptive design mindset where capabilities are recognized, built, bundled, and applied in a continuous organization designing process that optimizes those capabilities in practice. This adaptive designing and redesigning process has to be appreciated for what it is—a dynamic alignment engine that requires embracing change and continuous investments in capacity building. Risk management also has to become an organization-wide activity where the value/cost/risk calculations can be done quickly and efficiently in order to manage exposure relative to opportunity.

Finally, the organization needs to learn how to play well with others in its ecosystem, and the CHRO helps here too. Collaborative skills needed for effective participation in alliances, joint ventures, research consortia, industry federations, and coalitions need to be top-notch in a globalizing economy in which partners are temporary and quickly change. In many technology-intensive industries, this has been the case for decades, but smaller, younger companies are now engaging in collaborative ventures at an unprecedented pace and these skills are not as highly developed for them.

Assessing AR

The Appendix includes a survey instrument with which you can assess agility and resiliency dimensions in your organization at all four levels. Items have been selected to fit within each cell of the 4×5 matrix in Chapter Three. We provide it for application in your organization, *not* for commercial use by consultants in any form. This instrument is based on what we derived in our initial research and therefore adopts items from previously statistically validated research samples composed of several hundred organizations across multiple industries and nations. Other items have been added that are derived from other scholarly studies and through our own intensive work sessions with large groups of senior HR professionals and executives over a five-year period. These items comprise a short instrument that has not been statistically validated in its current form. We welcome opportunities to build, with the help of readers, a database that can do so. The survey is designed in three parts that try to capture the respondents' perceptions about their larger environment, their orientation toward change, and then perceptions across levels and five capabilities (three items per cell in the 4 × 5 matrix).

Several considerations about the survey need noting as you use it. First, multiple levels must be considered for all the reasons stressed in this book. What you are looking for is the alignment or consistency of scores across levels, not just the magnitude of those scores (that is, how high or low a mean value may be for an item). Statistically, the variability of those scores is also important as that is an indicator of consensus or ambiguity. This is true at individual, team, and organizations levels. Consistent with our terminology throughout the book, we use the term ecosystem in the survey and define it, but we caution that it could be confusing to respondents who haven't read the entire book.

Second, comparisons between scores associated with each of the capabilities should be made to determine whether some or all are aligned with each other—that is, whether one or another score was notably higher or lower than others. Third, scores should be matched or correlated with specific performance metrics or work outcomes to determine whether there are relationships between capabilities and measurable outcomes. The usual caveats apply, namely to beware of attributing cause and effect to such relationships. Leads and lags in causes and effects are notorious factors that distort such performance comparisons. Please, look for patterns, but do not draw firm conclusions based on one survey or a small sample.

Instead, we advise getting a benchmark reading of your organization by collecting survey data from a wide sample of employees. The data's greatest value also comes when assessments are made over time. The results from an initial assessment can then be compared with subsequent ones that will help focus specific interventions to improve specific capabilities. Regular scans should be scheduled, but it's also important for you to do an assessment after a particularly significant high-impact event or experience. Those become valuable opportunities to assess the resiliency of the organization in terms of response time and identify sources of any changes in scores.

We would be pleased to provide advice in your survey research design efforts, or your own internal staff, consultants, and local academics can assist you. The goal is to improve agility and resiliency and we are pleased to help accomplish that shared goal. Our website (www.HighAR.com) also contains additional survey items and facilitates analysis visually.

Conclusion

We have tried to make the case for a sophisticated, multifaceted analysis of environmental turbulence in terms of its causes and effects on individuals, teams, organizations, and their ecosystems. Turbulence is unlikely to subside. We even suggested that it is becoming the "new normal." It is challenging enough to think of operating effectively at the current levels of volatility being experienced by businesses and governments around the world. Unfortunately, the realistic prospect is that it will continue to accelerate, not hold steady or diminish. That's the bad news we feel compelled to deliver.

But the good news is that we wrote this book because we understand that adaptive capacity can be built to the point where turbulence can also provide opportunity, not just threats. Building agility and resiliency together and across levels is, we believe, the way out. These are complex, often confusing concepts and the five capabilities explored in this book may help give you the leverage to first understand, and, second, begin designing and executing interventions to build those capabilities.

Use our concepts and ideas to start making sense of some of the things you observe in your own organization. Read more to deepen your knowledge, and engage in discussions with others in seminars and other forums about how to use the concepts and ideas. Some of the recommendations in this book, such as those related to knowledge management systems, require a great deal of time, attention, and financial investment, so it is important to establish a strategic plan that addresses those resource concerns. Our suggested interventions are not just demands for additional resources. For instance, if a health and wellness plan is introduced and actually generates documented cost savings, perhaps those savings can become a source of investment in other AR development initiatives.

Time to get creative. Time to get moving.

appendix

Assessing Agility and Resiliency

This survey is designed as the basis for an AR assessment within your organization. One of the keys in building adaptive capacity is balancing attention between agility and resiliency at multiple levels—individual, team, organization, and ecosystem. Although many measures exist for agility and resiliency, we found that the following items can give an accurate snapshot of where you, your team, your organization, and your ecosystem are in terms of AR capacity. Many of the items have been empirically validated for assessing AR (AMA/HRI, 2006; McCann, Selsky, & Lee, 2009) whereas other items have long histories of use in change management research. We also plan to test them in additional research.

Getting factual data from surveys such as this is always helpful for testing qualitative judgments and opinions of individuals. In this book we have strongly advocated creating metrics and dashboards that monitor shifts in the force, frequency, and direction of things to backstop perceptions. This is part of building the capability of Being Aware. Nonetheless, perception-based survey data is useful because empirical studies have found that the perceptions of highly experienced and well-situated individuals can correlate strongly with perceptions of such measures as organization competitiveness. Perception data gives you indicators of where to look more closely if specific items in the survey are out of line with the overall pattern of responses. Such data help provide a starting point for serious inquiry and development.

Here is a short form of a more comprehensive instrument found on our website (www.HighAR.com). It parallels the 4×5 matrix in Chapter Three, with its twenty cells, consisting of three questions for each level for each capability, totaling sixty questions in Part C. The comprehensive online version offers a user-friendly interface and visually appealing presentation of results for a single respondent. The version offered in this appendix provides the basis for creating a standardized survey that could be administered to large numbers of respondents and then statistically analyzed.

There is no restriction on the application of this instrument other than that you maintain high professional standards, as you would any survey, and that you provide an appropriate, visible citation for its source. Its use is *not* permitted for commercial purposes in all or in parts by consultants. We welcome the opportunity to assist users of the survey to interpret results on a confidential basis. As academic scholars, we want to better understand what is happening in organizations and view this as an opportunity for us as well as you to learn.

The survey is designed in several parts that capture a respondent's (a) perceptions about the external environment, (b) orientation toward change, and (c) perceptions relating to the five capabilities discussed in this book. An additional section (d) concerning perceptions across the four levels is included in the Web version. This aids in checking for overall alignment and consistency. You would likely add demographic items relevant to your organization such as position title, time in position, location, and so forth to categorize respondents for analysis.

*In Parts A and B please complete the following questions by **circling** the letter next to the one statement in each numbered item that best describes your experience:*

Part A—Assessing Perceptions About the Environment

1. We define the *pace of change* as variations in the frequency, number, and kinds of conditions you experience. Compared to the past five years, which statement best describes the *pace of change* your organization now experiences?
   a. The pace is actually slower—briefer periods of significant change
   b. The pace is about the same and still predictable
   c. The pace is faster but still predictable
   d. The pace is very much faster and increasingly unpredictable
   e. The pace is extremely fast—it is impossible to predict what will happen next

2. We define disruptive change as severe surprises and unantici- pated shocks that may significantly destabilize your organization. Compared to the past five years, which statement best describes the disruptiveness your organization now experiences?
   a. Fewer and less frequent shocks and surprises than before
   b. About the same number and frequency of shocks and surprises
   c. More shocks and surprises
   d. Many more shocks and surprises
   e. Very many more shocks and surprises

3. In the past twelve months, has your organization experienced disruptive change—a surprise or unanticipated shock?
   a. No
   b. Yes—only minor disruption and operational impact
   c. Yes—core operations were impacted
   d. Yes—a major business strategy shift was required
   e. Yes—our overall mission and vision was challenged
   f. Yes—our long-term viability and existence was/is threatened

(Continued)

4. If you responded "Yes" to #3, then, all things considered, how effectively has your organization managed this disruption?
   a. Not effectively at all
   b. Very ineffectively
   c. Somewhat effectively
   d. Very effectively
   e. Exceptionally effectively

Part B—Assessing Your Orientation Toward Change

5. Which of the following statements is most descriptive of your organization?
   a. We induce change and force others to react
   b. We anticipate and plan for change before it happens
   c. We are the first to react once change occurs
   d. We first watch how others react, then react
   e. We are not fast or effective in reacting

6. How does your organization generally view change?
   a. As an opportunity—we like things shaken up
   b. As normal—expected and manageable
   c. As a threat—destabilizes what we do
   d. As wearing us down—too much for too long
   e. As overwhelming—beyond our ability to manage

Part C—Assessing Capabilities

Definitions:

My team/group means the one that you work in most frequently.

My organization means that business unit or operating division that you work in.

My ecosystem means the set of organizations and groups around your business unit with which you directly interact.

Use the following scale to indicate how you generally perceive or feel about each of the items in the list that follows. Place a number from the scale in the space to the right of each item.

0	1	2	3	4	5
Don't Know	Not at All	Very Little	Somewhat	Very Much	Completely

Being Purposeful

1. My organization's products and services are valuable and distinctive. ____

2. My team/group is flexible and adaptable to change. ____

3. People in this organization generally care about being healthy. ____

4. I have a strong sense of who I am and my values/beliefs. ____

5. I function very well during prolonged pressure and stress. ____

6. I understand and fully share my organization's values and beliefs. ____

7. My team/group has a strong shared sense of identity and values/beliefs. ____

8. My team/group shares the organization's values and beliefs. ____

9. My organization has a strong identity and purpose that can survive anything. ____

10. My ecosystem has healthy and thriving competitors, customers, and suppliers. ____

11. Our industry or ecosystem is well regarded and valued by society. ____

12. Members in our industry or ecosystem have widely shared values and beliefs. ____

Being Aware

13. We know and focus on the big challenges facing this organization. ____

(Continued)

14. My team/group members actively share information and ideas.   ____

15. Our industry actively monitors trends and issues affecting its members.   ____

16. I am an active learner about new ideas and issues.   ____

17. I am not often surprised by events or changes.   ____

18. Members of our ecosystem share what they know with each other.   ____

19. In general, learning is encouraged in this organization.   ____

20. My team/group is good at making sense of ambiguous, uncertain situations.   ____

21. My team/group has deep experience—we've seen and done it all.   ____

22. I am good at making sense of ambiguous, uncertain situations.   ____

23. My organization is good at making sense of ambiguous, uncertain situations.   ____

24. In this ecosystem members know and focus on the big challenges facing them.   ____

Being Action-Oriented

25. Change is expected and encouraged in this organization.   ____

26. My organization works hard in developing its most valuable capabilities.   ____

27. My organization is very entrepreneurial and moves quickly to create advantage.   ____

28. I recognize and take calculated risks when necessary.   ____

29. We form and re-form teams and groups as needed in this organization.   ____

30. I am open to change.   ____

31. I have the training and skills needed to perform very well. ____

32. My team/workgroup is open to change. ____

33. My team/workgroup has the training and skills we need to perform very well. ____

34. My organization bounces back quickly from adversity or unexpected events. ____

35. My ecosystem is known for rapid responses to change by major players. ____

36. My ecosystem's key players collaborate well in dealing with shared challenges. ____

Being Resourceful

37. My team/group is willing to try new ways of doing things. ____

38. My organization is good at improvising—creating new ways of doing things. ____

39. Our teams have clear, well-rehearsed roles/responsibilities for crisis situations. ____

40. My organization invests the resources needed to stay creative and innovative. ____

41. I am able to keep my skills and knowledge current. ____

42. My organization is good at deploying and redeploying resources across teams. ____

43. Our industry members can access the resources needed to meet any challenge. ____

44. My ecosystem has deep talent for dealing with issues that members share. ____

45. I always try to find creative solutions to problems. ____

46. I think of myself as very entrepreneurial. ____

(Continued)

47. My organization is good at quickly deploying and redeploying resources.   ____

48. My ecosystem is creative in dealing with opportunities and threats.   ____

Being Networked

49. I have good personal networks with others around this organization.   ____

50. My organization "prunes" network relationships to manage them.   ____

51. We never let boundaries between teams get in the way of doing things.   ____

52. I have access to the resources needed to perform very well.   ____

53. I have access to key decision makers and leaders as needed.   ____

54. My team/group has the resources needed to perform very well.   ____

55. My team/group has access to key decision makers and leaders as needed.   ____

56. My organization has a strong network of external alliances and partnerships.   ____

57. My organization has access to the capital and resources to weather anything.   ____

58. Our ecosystem is supported by strong professional networks and associations.   ____

59. We have tightly linked and durable supply chains for sourcing and delivering.   ____

60. Our ecosystem can access the capital and resources for managing change.   ____

Scoring and Interpreting the Results

Parts A and B—Perceptions About the Environment and Orientations Toward Change

Responses in Parts A and B can be used to obtain an overall assessment of employee views regarding the environment and change. They can also be used to classify the surveys into subgroups to assess the patterns of responses to Part C. More advanced statistical analyses (correlations, regressions) may be possible depending upon the number of respondents involved.

Part C—Assessing Capabilities

Each subsection represents a capability. Add all responses within each subsection and divide as follows to get the respondent's average perception for each capability:

- Being Purposeful: _____/12* = _____

- Being Aware: _____/12* = _____

- Being Action-Oriented: _____/12* = _____

- Being Resourceful: _____/12* = _____

- Being Networked: _____/12* = _____

- Overall AR Score (sum of 5 average capability scores): _____

   Respondent scores: Average scores for a capability could range from 1.0 to 5.0, assuming "0" responses are eliminated. Two types of analysis are possible with these data. First, a specific capability average can be compared to the prevailing level of change being experienced. Second, if many respondents' average scores between capabilities differ by more than 1.0, then it is important to engage in additional inquiry, whether through survey research or interviews with respondents, to try to ascertain why those differences may exist.

*If there are 0 responses, drop those responses and then reduce the denominator accordingly.

(*Continued*)

It may be due to a lack of knowledge about conditions or it may be due to legitimate beliefs that such differences do actually exist. If believed legitimate, then interventions specifically designed to improve lower scored areas may be called for. The overall AR score is calculated by summing the five capability average scores.

Aggregate scores: You can calculate averages across the organization for each capability by summing and averaging the capability scores for all respondents. The same can be done for the overall AR score. You could also calculate averages for each capability by unit (for example, marketing, production, European division, software division), and for the overall AR score, and compare scores across units.

Examine the distribution of overall AR Capability scores across all respondents. A score of 20–25 is a strong indicator of High AR. A score of 12–19 indicates a moderate level of AR. A score of 5–11 indicates serious issues concerning AR, for which interventions should be immediately considered after understanding the specific sources that contributed to the low score. Obviously, the "right" level of AR depends on the level of prevailing levels of turbulence in the environment, so comparisons to other measures (such as correlations in larger group surveys) are recommended.

As noted at the beginning of this appendix, the survey responses are intended as a starting point for additional discussion and inquiry. We encourage creative uses of this instrument.

REFERENCES

ABI Research. (2011, February). Telepresence and videoconferencing equipment market: MCUs, gateways, gatekeepers, single-codec and multi-codec endpoints, executive desktops and desktop videoconferencing (Tech.). Retrieved from http://www.abiresearch.com/research/1003771

Ackoff, R. L. (2010). *Systems thinking for curious managers.* Devon, UK: Triarchy Press.

Allison, G. T., & Zelikow, P. (1999). *Essence of decision: Explaining the Cuban Missile Crisis.* New York: Longman.

Amabile, T. M. (2007). How to kill creativity. *Harvard Business Review Executive Edition*, (Spring), 50–64.

Amabile, T. M., Hadley, C. N., & Kramer, S. (2007). Creativity under the gun. *Harvard Business Review Executive*, (Spring), 36–46.

American Management Association/Human Resources Institute (AMA/HRI). (2006). Agility and resiliency in the face of continuous change: Report of a global study of current trends and future possibilities 2006–2016. New York: American Management Association.

Aon Hewitt. (2011). Aon Hewitt's 2011 talent survey: Igniting a high-performance culture (Rep.). Retrieved from www.aonhewitt.com

Argyris, C. (1986). Reinforcing organizational defensive routines: An unintended human resources activity. *Human Resource Management*, 25(4), 541–555. doi:10.1002/hrm.3930250405

Argyris, C. (1994). Good communication that blocks learning. *Harvard Business Review*, July, 72(4), 77–85.

Argyris, C., & Schön, D. (1978). *Organizational learning: A theory of action perspective.* Reading, MA: Addison Wesley.

Aron, R., & Singh, J. V. (2005). Getting offshoring right. *Harvard Business Review*, December, 135–143.

Ashby, W. R. (1956). *An introduction to cybernetics.* New York: Wiley.

Bacharach, S., Bamberger, P., & McKinney, V. (2000). Boundary management tactics and logics of action: The case of peer support providers. *Administrative Science Quarterly, 45,* 704–736.

Barney, J. (1991). Firm resources and sustained competitive advantage. *Journal of Management, 17*(1), 99–120.

Barthelemy, J. (2003). The seven deadly sins of outsourcing. *Academy of Management Executive, 17*(2), 87–100.

Berardino, J. Television interview on CNBC, December 2, 3011.

Berry, L. L., Mirabito, A. M., & Baun, W. B. (2010). What's the hard return on employee wellness programs. *Harvard Business Review,* December, *88*(12), 104–112.

Bialik, C. (2009, July 29). Marriage-maker claims are tied in knots. *The Wall Street Journal.*

Birkinshaw, J., & Gibson, C. (2004). Building ambidexterity into an organization. *MIT Sloan Management Review,* Summer, 47–55.

Blanchard, D. (2010). *Supply chain management: Best practices.* Hoboken, NJ: Wiley.

Blanchard, K., & Barrett, C. (2010). *Lead with luv: A different way to create real success.* Upper Saddle River, NJ: Pearson Education.

Bonabeau, E. (2007). Understanding and managing complexity risk. *MIT Sloan Management Review,* Summer, 62–68.

Bouchikhi, H., & Kimberly, J. R. (2003). Escaping the identity trap. *MIT Sloan Management Review,* Spring, 20–26.

Boyatzis, R. E., & Akrivou, K. (2006). The ideal self as a driver of change. *Journal of Management Development, 25*(7), 624–642.

Brown, G. (2010). *Beyond the crash: Overcoming the first crisis of globalization.* New York: Free Press.

Brown, S., & Eisenhardt, K. (1997). The art of continuous change: Linking complexity theory and time-paced evolution in relentlessly shifting organizations. *Administrative Science Quarterly, 42,* 1–34.

Brown, S. L., & Eisenhardt, K. M. (1998). *Competing on the edge: Strategy as structured chaos.* Boston: Harvard Business School Press.

Buettner, D. (2010). *Thrive: Finding happiness the Blue Zones way.* Washington: National Geographic Society.

Cameron, K. S., Dutton, J. E., & Quinn, R. E. (2003). Foundations of positive organizational scholarship. In K. Cameron, J. E. Dutton, & R. E. Quinn (Eds.), *Positive organizational scholarship.* San Francisco: Berrett-Koehler, 3–13.

Carr, N. (2010, June). Chaos theory. *Wired,* 112–118.

Casti, J. L. (2010). *Mood matters: From rising skirt lengths to the collapse of world powers.* New York: Copernicus Books.

Chesbrough, H. W. (2003). *Open innovation the new imperative for creating and profiting from technology.* Boston: Harvard Business School Press.

Christensen, C. M. (1997). *The innovator's dilemma: When new technologies cause great firms to fail.* Boston: Harvard Business School Press.

Christensen, C. M., & Overdorf, M. (2000). Meeting the challenges of disruptive change. *Harvard Business Review, 78*(2), 66–67.

Christopher, M. (2005). *Logistics and supply chain management: Creating value-added networks.* Harlow, UK: FT Prentice Hall.

Churchland, P. S. (2011). *Braintrust: What neuroscience tells us about morality.* Princeton, NJ: Princeton University Press.

Coff, R., & Kryscynski, D. (2011). Invited editorial: Drilling for micro-foundations of human capital-based competitive advantages. *Journal of Management, 37*(5), 1429–1443. doi:10.1177/0149206310397772

Cohen, B. (1983). The planner as reticulist: Network interventions in a human services setting (Unpublished doctoral dissertation). University of Pennsylvania.

Cohen, R. (2010). The new American normal. *New York Times* online. Retrieved from http://www.nytimes.com/2010/09/28/opinion/28iht-edcohen.html

Colbert, A. E., Kristof-Brown, A. L., Bradley, B. H., & Barrick, M. R. (2008). CEO transformational leadership: The role of goal importance congruence in top management teams. *Academy of Management Journal, 51*(1), 81–96.

Collins, J. C., & Porras, J. I. (2002). *Built to last: Successful habits of visionary companies.* New York: HarperBusiness Essentials.

Coutu, D. (2002). How resilience works. *Harvard Business Review, 80*(5), 46–55.

Covey, S. R. (2004). *The 8th habit: From effectiveness to greatness.* New York: Free Press.

Cross, R., Hargadon, A., Parise, S., & Thomas, R. (2007). Together we innovate. *MIT Sloan Management Review,* September. Retrieved from http://sloanreview.mit.edu/executive-adviser/2007–4/49412/together-we-innovate/

Crossan, M. M. (1998). Improvisation in action. *Organization Science, 9*(5), 593–599. doi:10.1287/orsc.9.5.593

D'Aveni, R. A. (1994). With R. Gunther. *Hypercompetition: Managing the dynamics of strategic maneuvering.* New York: Free Press.

Davenport, T. H., & Prusak, L. (1998). *Working knowledge: How organizations manage what they know.* Boston: Harvard Business School Press.

de Geus, A. (1997). *The living company.* Boston: Harvard Business School Press.

Dean, D., & Webb, C. (2011). Recovering from information overload. *McKinsey Quarterly*, January, 3–10. Retrieved from www.mckinsey quarterly.com/Recovering_from_information_overload_2735

Delapierre, M., & Mytelka, L. (1998). Blurring boundaries: New inter-firm relationships and the emergence of networked, knowledge-based oligopolies. In M. Colombo (ed.) *The changing boundaries of the firm: Explaining evolving inter-firm relations* (pp. 73–94). London: Routledge.

Dewhurst, M., Harris, J., & Heywood, S. (2011). Understanding your "globalization penalty." *McKinsey Quarterly*, July, issue 3, 12–15.

Drucker, P. F. (1969). *The age of discontinuity*. Oxford: Butterworth-Heinemann.

Drucker, P. F. (1973). *Management*. New York: Harper.

Drucker, P. F. (1985). *Innovation and entrepreneurship: Practice and principles*. New York: Harper & Row.

Eckersley, R. (2008). Nihilism, fundamentalism, or activism: Three responses to fears of the Apocalypse. *The Futurist*, January–February, 35–39.

Edvinsson, L., & Malone, M. S. (1997). *Intellectual capital: Realizing your company's true value by finding its hidden brainpower*. New York: Harper Collins.

Efstathiou, J., & Chipman, K. (2010). As temperatures rise, business adapts. *Bloomberg Business Week*, December 13–19, 25.

Eisenhardt, K. M., & Galunic, D. C. (2000). Coevolving: At last, a way to make synergies work. *Harvard Business Review*, 28(1), 91–101.

Eisenhardt, K. M., & Martin, J. A. (2000). Dynamic capabilities: What are they? *Strategic Management Journal*, *21*(10–11), 1105–1121. doi: 10.1002/1097–0266(200010/11)21:10/113.0.CO;2-E

Eldridge, T. R., Ginsburg, S., Hempel, W. T., II, Kephart, J. L., & Moore, K. (2004, August 21). *9/11 and terrorist travel: Staff report of the National Commission on Terrorist Attacks upon the United States (Rep.)*. Retrieved from govinfo.library.unt.edu/911/staff_statements/index.htm

Emery, F. E., & Trist, E. L. (1965). The causal texture of organizational environments. *Human Relations*, *18*(1), 21–32. doi:10.1177/001872676501800103

Ernst, C., & Chrobot-Mason, D. (2011). *Boundary spanning leadership: Six practices for solving problems, driving innovation, and transforming organizations*. New York: McGraw-Hill.

Fink, A., & Vickers, M. (Eds.). (2011). Special issue: Using human capital analytics to make excellent business decisions. *People and Strategy*, *34*(2).

Florida, R. L. (2005). *The flight of the creative class: The new global competition for talent*. New York: HarperBusiness.

Florida, R. L. (2010). *The great reset: How new ways of living and working drive post-crash prosperity.* New York: Harper.

Ford, M. (2009). *The lights in the tunnel: Automation, accelerating technology and the economy of the future.* Acculant Publishing. Retrieved from www.Acculant.com

Frankl, V. E. (1959/1984). *Man's search for meaning: An introduction to logotherapy.* New York: Simon & Schuster.

Freeman, S. F., Hirschhorn, L., & Maltz, M. (2004). The power of moral purpose: Sandler O'Neill & partners in the aftermath of September 11, 2001. *Organization Development Journal, 22*(4), 69–81.

Freiberg, K., & Freiberg, J. (1996). *Nuts!: Southwest Airlines' crazy recipe for business and personal success.* Austin, TX: Bard Books.

Friedman, T. L. (2005). *The world is flat: A brief history of the twenty-first century.* New York: Farrar, Straus and Giroux.

Frost, P. J. (2007). *Toxic emotions at work and what you can do about them.* Boston: Harvard Business School Press.

Galbraith, J. R. (1995). *Designing organizations: An executive briefing on strategy, structure, and process.* San Francisco: Jossey-Bass.

Galbraith, J. R. (2009). *Designing matrix organizations that actually work: How IBM, Procter & Gamble, and others design for success.* San Francisco: Jossey-Bass.

Galbraith, J. R., Downey, D., & Kates, A. (2002). *Designing dynamic organizations: A hands-on guide for leaders at all levels.* New York: AMACOM.

Gallup-Healthways (2009, May). Workplace wellness, behavioral economics. Daily News, Polls, Public Opinion on Government, Politics, Economics, Management. Retrieved from http://www.gallup.com/poll/wellbeing.aspx

George, B., & Sims, P. (2007). *True north: Discover your authentic leadership.* San Francisco: Jossey-Bass.

Goldfarb, R. W. (2011, May 15). Preoccupations: When fear stifles initiative. *New York Times,* p. 8.

Gossieaux, F., & Moran, E. (2011). *The hyper-social organization: Eclipse your competition by leveraging social media.* New York: McGraw-Hill.

Gray, B. (1985). Conditions facilitating interorganizational collaboration. *Human Relations, 38*(10), 911–936. doi:10.1177/0018726785038 01001

Grove, A. S. (1996). *Only the paranoid survive.* London: Profile Books.

Hamel, G., & Välikangas, L. (2003). The quest for resilience. *Harvard Business Review, 81*(9), 52–63.

Hansen, M. T., & Birkinshaw, J. (2007). The innovation value chain. *Harvard Business Review,* June, 121–130.

Hart, S. L. (2010). *Capitalism at the crossroads: Next generation business strategies for a post-crisis world.* (3rd ed.) Upper Saddle River, NJ: Wharton School Publishing.

Hartung, J., & Nagireddy, C. (2010). Trauma in organizations: Prevention and treatment with emergent strategies from alternative psychology. *Journal of Psychological Issues in Organizational Culture, 1*(1), 29–59. doi:10.1002/jpoc.20007

Hedberg, B. (1980). How organizations learn and unlearn. In P. C. Nystrom and W. H. Starbuck (Eds.), *Handbook of organizational design,* Vol. 1. Oxford: Oxford University Press, 3–27.

Herbst, P. (1974). *Socio-technical design.* London: Tavistock.

Hirschhorn, L. (1997). *Reworking authority: Leading and following in the post-modern organization.* Cambridge, MA: MIT Press.

Hirschhorn, L., & Gilmore, T. (1992). The new boundaries of the "boundaryless" company. *Harvard Business Review,* May–June, 104–115.

Homer-Dixon, T. F. (2006). *The upside of down: Catastrophe, creativity, and the renewal of civilization.* Washington, DC: Island Press.

Horney, N., Pasmore, B., & O'Shea, T. (2010). Leadership agility: A business imperative for a VUCA world. *People and Strategy, 33*(4), 32–38.

Hsu, D., & Lim, K. (2006, July 12). In biotech startups, knowledge bridging can be the key to creativity. *Knowledge@Wharton.* Retrieved from http://knowledge.wharton.upenn.edu/article.cfm?articleid=1518

Hutchins, E. (1995). *Cognition in the wild.* Cambridge, MA: MIT Press.

Huy, Q. N., & Mintzberg, H. (2003). The rhythm of change. *MIT Sloan Management Review,* Summer, 79–84.

Iansiti, M., & Levien, R. (2004). Strategy as ecology. *Harvard Business Review, 82,* March, 69–78.

Institute for Corporate Productivity (i4cp). (2011). *The 2011 five domains of high performance (Rep.).* Retrieved from www.i4cp.com

Iyer, A. V., Seshadri, S., & Vasher, R. (2009). *Toyota supply chain management: A strategic approach to the principles of Toyota's renowned system.* New York: McGraw-Hill.

Iyer, B., Lee, C.-H., & Venkatraman, N. (2006). Managing in a "small world ecosystem": Lessons from the software industry. *California Management Review, 48*(3), 28–47.

Jackall, R. (1988). *Moral mazes: The world of corporate managers.* Oxford: Oxford University Press.

Jargon, J. (2011, November 11). Latest Starbucks concoction: Juice. *Wall Street Journal,* B1–B2.

Johnson, J. (2011, March). My gadget guilt. *Wired,* 94–103. Retrieved from http://www.wired.com/about/2011/03/19–03-march-2011-highlights-2/

Kansas, D. (2009). *The end of Wall Street as we know it.* New York: Wall Street Journal Press.

Kanter, R. M. (1994). Collaborative advantage: The art of alliances. *Harvard Business Review,* July–August, 96–108.

Kanter, R. M. (2003). Leadership and the psychology of turnarounds. *Harvard Business Review,* June, *81*(6), 58–67.

Karlgaard, R., & Gilder, G. (1996, February 26). Talking with Intel's Andy Grove. *Forbes,* 63.

Kay, J. (2011). *Among the truthers: A journey through America's growing conspiracist underground.* New York: Harper.

Kelley, T., & Littman, J. (2001). *The art of innovation: Lessons in creativity from IDEO, America's leading design firm.* New York: Currency/Doubleday.

Kelley, T., & Littman, J. (2005). *The ten faces of innovation: IDEO's strategies for beating the devil's advocate & driving creativity throughout your organization.* New York: Currency/Doubleday.

Kesler, G., & Kates, A. (2010). *Leading organization design: How to make organization design decisions to drive the results you want.* San Francisco: Jossey-Bass.

Key, M., Thompson, H., & McCann, J. (2009). Knowledge management: A glass half full. *People and Strategy, 32*(4), 42–47.

Kidder, T. (1981). *The soul of a new machine.* Boston: Little, Brown.

Koerner, B. I. (2011, March). Made in the USA. *Wired,* 105–109.

Koestler, A. (1964). *The act of creation.* New York: Macmillan.

Kurtz, C. F., & Snowden, D. J. (2003). The new dynamics of strategy: Sense-making in a complex and complicated world. *IBM Systems Journal, 42*(3), 462–483. doi:10.1147/sj.423.0462

Lawler, E. E., III, & Worley, C. G. (2011). *Management reset: Organizing for sustainable effectiveness.* San Francisco: Jossey-Bass.

Lengnick-Hall, C. A., & Beck, T. E. (2009). Resilience capacity and strategic agility: Prerequisites for thriving in a dynamic environment. In C. P. Nemeth, E. Hollnagel, & S. Dekker (Eds.), *Resilience engineering perspectives,* Vol. 2 (pp. 39–69). Farnham, UK: Ashgate.

Lévi-Strauss, C. (1966). *The savage mind.* Chicago: University of Chicago Press.

Levy, S. (2011, February). Inside Google Plus. *Wired.* Retrieved from www.wired.com/magazine/2011/09/ff_google_horowitz/all/1

Lichtenthaler, U., & Lichtenthaler, E. (2009). A capability-based framework for open innovation: Complementing absorptive capacity. *Journal of Management Studies, 46*(8), 1315–1338. doi:10.1111/j.1467–6486 .2009.00854.x

Lynn, M. L. (2005). Organizational buffering: Managing boundaries and cores. *Organization Studies, 26*(1), 37–61. doi:10.1177/01708406 05046348

Madsen, S., & Vance, C. (2009). Unlearned lessons from the past: An insider's view of Enron's downfall. *Corporate Governance, 9*(2), 217–227.

Manyika, J. (2011). Google's CFO on growth, capital structure, and leadership. *McKinsey Quarterly*, August, 1–7.

Marot, M., Selsky, J. W., Hart, W., & Reddy, P. (2005). Collaborating through a consortium: The role of intellectual property in an Australian biotechnology field. *Advances in Interdisciplinary Studies of Work Teams, 11*, 1–31.

Masley, S. (2005). *Ten years younger: The amazing ten-week plan to look better, feel better, and turn back the clock.* New York: Broadway Books.

May, T. A. (2009). *The new know: Innovation powered by analytics.* Hoboken, NJ: Wiley.

McCann, J. E. (1983). Design guidelines for social problem-solving interventions. *The Journal of Applied Behavioral Science, 19*(2), 177–189. doi:10.1177/002188638301900213

McCann, J. E. (1990). *Sweet success: How NutraSweet created a billion dollar business.* Homewood, IL: Irwin.

McCann, J. E. (2004, March). Organizational effectiveness: Changing concepts for changing environments. *Human Resource Planning Journal*, 42–50.

McCann, J. E., & Buckner, M. (2004). Strategically integrating knowledge management initiatives. *Journal of Knowledge Management*, 8.

McCann, J. E., & Gilkey, R. (1988). *Joining forces: Creating and managing successful mergers and acquisitions.* New York: Prentice Hall.

McCann, J. E., & Gomez-Mejia, L. (1990). Exploring the dimensions of an international social issues climate. *Human Relations, 43*(2), 141–167. doi:10.1177/001872679004300204

McCann, J. E., & Selsky, J. W. (1984). Hyperturbulence and the emergence of type 5 environments. *Academy of Management Review, 9*(3), 460–470.

McCann, J. E., & Selsky, J. W. (2003, August). Boundary formation, defense, and destruction: Strategically managing environmental turbulence. Academy of Management national meetings, Seattle.

McCann, J. E., Selsky, J. W., & Lee, J. (2009). Building agility, resiliency and performance in turbulent environments. *People & Strategy, 32*(3), 44–51.

McLean, B., & Elkind, P. (2003). *The smartest guys in the room: The amazing rise and scandalous fall of Enron.* New York: Penguin.

Menzies-Lyth, I. (1990) Social systems as a defense against anxiety: An empirical study of the nursing service of a general hospital. In E. Trist & H. Murray (Eds.), *The social engagement of social science: A Tavistock anthology*, Vol. 1 (pp. 439–462). Philadelphia: The University of Pennsylvania Press.

Meyer, A. D. (1982). Adapting to environmental jolts. *Administrative Science Quarterly, 27*, 515–537.

Meyer, A. D., Goes, J. B., & Brooks, G. R. (1993). Organizations reacting to hyperturbulence. In G. Huber & W. Glick (Eds.), *Organizational change and redesign: Ideas and insights for improving performance* (pp. 66–111). New York: Oxford University Press.

Mihm, S. (2008, August 15). Eight who saw it coming. *Fortune.*

Mitroff, I. I. (2002). Crisis learning: The lessons of failure. *The Futurist,* September–October, 19–21.

Mitroff, I. I., & Alpaslan, M. C. (2003). Preparing for evil. *Harvard Business Review*, April, 109–115.

Nadler, D. (1992). Organizational architecture: A metaphor for change. In *Organizational architecture: Designs for changing organizations* (pp. 1–8). San Francisco: Jossey-Bass.

Nocera, J. (2006, September 9). After 5 years, his voice can still crack. *New York Times*, C1.

Nonaka, I. (1991). The knowledge-creating company. *Harvard Business Review, 69*(6), Nov–Dec, 96–104.

Nonaka, I., & Takeuchi, H. (1995). *The knowledge-creating company: How Japanese companies create the dynamics of innovation.* New York: Oxford University Press.

Normann, R., & Ramirez, R. (1993). From value chain to value constellation: Designing interactive strategy. *Harvard Business Review, 71,* July–August, 65–77.

Parker, B., & Selsky, J. W. (2004). Interface dynamics in cause-based partnerships: An exploration of emergent culture. *Nonprofit and Voluntary Sector Quarterly, 33*(3), 458–488. doi:10.1177/0899764 004266016

Pearson, C. M., & Mitroff, I. I. (1993). From crisis prone to crisis prepared: A framework for crisis management. *Academy of Management Executive, 7*(1), 48–59.

Penenberg, A. L. (2011a, September). They have hacked your brain. *Fast Company*, 85–126.

Penenberg, A. L. (2011b, November). Innovator in chief. *Fast Company,* 78–84.

Perrow, C. (1984). *Normal accidents: Living with high-risk technologies.* New York: Basic Books.

Perrow, C. (2007). *The next catastrophe: Reducing our vulnerabilities to natural, industrial, and terrorist disasters.* Princeton, NJ: Princeton University Press.

Peters, T. J. (1987). *Thriving on chaos: Handbook for a management revolution.* New York: Knopf.

Peters, T. J. (1992). *Liberation management: Necessary disorganization for the nanosecond nineties.* New York: Ballantine.

Peters, T. J., & Waterman, R. H., Jr. (1982). *In search of excellence: Lessons from America's best-run companies.* New York: Harper & Row.

Pink, D. H. (2001). *Free agent nation: How America's new independent workers are transforming the way we live.* New York: Warner Books.

Pink, D. H. (2011). *Drive: The surprising truth about what motivates us.* New York: Riverhead Books.

Porac, J. F., Thomas, H., & Baden-Fuller, C. (2011). Competitive groups as cognitive communities: The case of Scottish knitwear manufacturers revisited. *Journal of Management Studies, 48*(3), 646–664. doi:10.1111/j.1467–6486.2010.00988.x

Porter, M. E. (1980). *Competitive strategy: Techniques for analyzing industries and competitors.* New York: Free Press.

Porter, M. E., & Kramer, M. R. (2011). Creating shared value: How to reinvent capitalism and unleash a wave of innovation and growth. *Harvard Business Review,* January–February, 62–77.

Putnam, H. (2009, November). Turbulence is inevitable . . . misery is optional: Ethics and integrity are your greatest assets in good times and in crisis. Bentley University Center for Business Ethics: Raytheon Lectureship in Business Ethics.

Putnam, R. D. (2000). *Bowling alone: The collapse and revival of community.* New York: Simon & Schuster.

Qualman, E. (2011). *Socialnomics: How social media transforms the way we live and do business.* Hoboken, NJ: Wiley.

Ramirez, R., Selsky, J. W., & Heijden, K. van der (eds.) (2010). *Business planning for turbulent times: New methods for applying scenarios.* London: Earthscan.

Reinmoeller, P., & Baardwijk, N. van (2005). The link between diversity and resilience. *MIT Sloan Management Review,* Summer, 61–65.

Retter, T. (2001, June). Technology forecast 2001–2003. Lecture presented by Price Waterhouse Coopers, Tampa, Florida.

Rheingold, H. (2002). *Smart mobs: The next social revolution.* Cambridge, MA: Perseus.

Robison, J. (2010). The business case for wellbeing. *The Gallup Management Journal,* June. doi:http://gmj.gallup.com/content/139373/Business-Case-Wellbeing.aspx

Rock, D. (2009). Managing with the brain in mind. *Oxford Leadership Journal, 1*(1), 1–10.

Rock, D. (2010). Impacting leadership with neuroscience. *People and Strategy, 33*(4), 6–11.

Santos, J., Doz, Y., & Williamson, P. (2004). Is your innovation process global? *MIT Sloan Management Review, 45*(4), 31–37.

Schultz, H. (2011). Advertisement. *New York Times,* September 4, p. 8.

Schumpeter, J. A., & Opie, R. (1934). *The theory of economic development: An inquiry into profits, capital, credit, interest, and the business cycle.* Cambridge, MA: Harvard University Press.

Schwab, K. (2011). A worldwide network for responding to the next crisis. *Harvard Business Review,* Jan–Feb, 56.

Seligman, M. (2011). *Flourish: A visionary new understanding of happiness and well-being.* New York: Free Press.

Selsky, J. W., & McCann, J. E. (2008). Managing disruptive change and turbulence through continuous change thinking and scenarios. In R. Ramirez, J. W. Selsky, & K. van der Heijden (Eds.), *Business planning for turbulent environments: New methods for applying scenarios* (pp. 167–186). London: Earthscan.

Selsky, J. W., & Parker, B. (2005). Cross-sector partnerships to address social issues: Challenges to theory and practice. *Journal of Management, 31*(6), 849–873.

Selsky, J. W., & Parker, B. (2010). Platforms for cross-sector social partnerships: Prospective sensemaking devices for social benefit. *Journal of Business Ethics, 94,* 21–37. doi:10.1007/s10551-011-0776-2

Senge, P. M. (1990). *The fifth discipline: The art and practice of the learning organization.* New York: Doubleday/Currency.

Senge, P. M. (2010). *The necessary revolution: Working together to create a sustainable world.* New York: Broadway Books.

Sennett, R. (2005). *The culture of the new capitalism.* New Haven, CT: Yale University Press.

Serrat, O. (2010). A primer on social neuroscience. *ADB, 89,* August. Retrieved from http://www.adb.org/documents/information/knowl edge-solutions/primer-on-social-neuroscience.pdf

Seyle, H. (1974). *Stress without distress.* Philadelphia: Lippincott.

Sheffi, Y. (2005). *The resilient enterprise: Overcoming vulnerability for competitive advantage.* Cambridge, MA: MIT Press.

Sheffi, Y., & Rice, J. B., Jr., (2005). A supply chain view of the resilient enterprise. *MIT Sloan Management Review, 47*(1), 41–48.

Sinek, S. (2009). *Start with why: How great leaders inspire everyone to take action.* New York: Portfolio Books/Penguin.

Sirmon, D. G., Hitt, M. A., & Ireland, R. D. (2007). Managing firm resources in dynamic environments to create value: Looking inside the black box. *Academy of Management Review, 32*(1), 273–292.

Sorkin, A. R. (2009). *Too big to fail: The inside story of how Wall Street and Washington fought to save the financial system—and themselves.* New York: Viking.

Staw, B., Sandelands, L., & Dutton, J. (1981). Threat-rigidity effects in organizational behavior. *Administrative Science Quarterly, 26,* December, 501–524.

Stewart, T. A. (1997). *Intellectual capital: The new wealth of organizations.* New York: Currency Doubleday.

Stix, G. (2011, March). The neuroscience of true grit. *Scientific American,* 29–33. Retrieved from http://ScientificAmerican.com

Sull, D. N. (2009). *The upside of turbulence: Seizing opportunity in an uncertain world.* New York: HarperBusiness.

Surowiecki, J. (2004). *The wisdom of crowds: Why the many are smarter than the few and how collective wisdom shapes business, economies, societies, and nations.* New York: Doubleday.

Sutcliffe, K. M. (1994). What executives notice: Accurate perceptions in top management teams. *Academy of Management Journal, 37*(5), 1360–1378.

Taleb, N. (2007). *The black swan: The impact of the highly improbable.* New York: Random House.

Taylor, F. W. (1911). *Principles of scientific management.* New York: Harper & Row.

Teece, D. J. (2007). Explicating dynamic capabilities: The nature and microfoundations of (sustainable) enterprise performance. *Strategic Management Journal, 28,* 1319–1350. doi:10.1002/smj.640

Teece, D. J. (2009). *Dynamic capabilities and strategic management: Organizing for innovation and growth.* Oxford: Oxford University Press.

Thompson, C. (2011, September). The breakthrough myth. *Fast Company,* 44.

Thompson, A., Strickland, A. J., & Gamble, J. E. (2010) *Crafting and executing strategy* (17th ed.). New York: McGraw-Hill.

Tischler, L. (2011, September). The design lessons of 9/11. *Fast Company,* 40–42.

Toffler, A., & Toffler, H. (1970). *Future shock.* New York: Random House.

Toffler, A., & Toffler, H. (1980). *The third wave.* New York: Morrow.

Topham, J. (2011, April 25). Japan quake jolts auto output, Toyota may fall to No. 3. *Reuters.* Retrieved from http://www.reuters.com/article/2011/04/25/autos-japan-production-idUSL3E7FP06P20110425

Towers Watson. (2011). Employer survey on purchasing value in health care. Retrieved from http://www.towerswatson.com/assets/pdf/3946 /TowersWatson-NBGH-2011-NA-2010–18560.pdf

Trist, E., Emery, F., & Murray, H. (Eds.). 1996. *The social engagement of social science: A Tavistock anthology*, Vol. III. Philadelphia: University of Pennsylvania Press.

Wack, P. (1995). Scenarios: Shooting the rapids. *Harvard Business Review*, Nov–Dec, 1–13.

Warren, R. (2002). *The purpose-driven life: What on earth am I here for?* Grand Rapids, MI: Zondervan.

Watkins, M. D., & Bazerman, M. H. (2003). Predictable surprises: The disasters you should have seen coming. *Harvard Business Review*, March, 72–80.

Weick, K. E. (1988). Enacted sensemaking in crisis situations. *Journal of Management Studies*, 25(4), 305–317.

Weick, K. E., & Sutcliffe, K. M. (2007). *Managing the unexpected: Resilient performance in an age of uncertainty.* San Francisco: Jossey-Bass.

Wenger, E. (1998). *Communities of practice: Learning, meaning, and identity.* Cambridge, UK: Cambridge University Press.

Whelan, E., Parise, S., DeValk, J., & Aalbers, R. (2011). Creating employee networks that deliver open innovation. *MIT Sloan Management Review*, *Fall*, 37–48.

Whitford, D. (Ed.). (2011). Sandler O'Neill's journey from Ground Zero. *Fortune*, September 5. Retrieved from http://management .fortune.cnn.com/2011/09/01/sandler-oneills-journey

Wildavsky, A. (1988). *Searching for safety.* Piscataway, NJ: Transaction Books.

Wilson, K., & Doz, Y. L. (2011). Agile innovation: A footprint balancing distance and immersion. *California Management Review*, 53(2), 6–26. doi:10.1525/cmr.2011.53.2.6

Wright, P. M., Pace, D. A., Boudreau, J. W., & Sartain, E. (2011). *The chief HR officer: Defining the new role of human resource leaders.* San Francisco: Jossey-Bass.

NAME INDEX

Page references followed by *e* indicate an exhibit.

K

Kansas, D., 28
Kanter, R. M., 52, 62, 156
Karlgaard, R., 27
Kates, A., 113, 134
Kay, J., 62
Kelleher, H., 79, 92–93
Kelley, T., 143
Kephart, J. L., 85
Kesler, G., 113
Key, M., 90
Kidder, T., 78
Kimberly, J. R., 11
Koerner, B. I., 125
Koestler, A., 132
Kramer, M. R., 43, 74
Kramer, S., 132
Kristof-Brown, A. L., 78
Kryscynski, D., 115, 116

L

Lawler, E. E., III, 119
Lay, K., 110
Lee, C-H., 158
Lee, J., 12, 19, 37
Lengnick-Hall, C., 130, 131
Lévi-Strauss, C., 130
Levien, R., 40, 159
Levy, S., 119
Lichtenthaler, E., 132
Lichtenthaler, U., 132
Lim, K., 94
Littman, J., 143
Lynn, M. L., 125

M

Madsen, S., 63, 109, 110
Malone, M. S., 88
Maltz, M., 55, 157
Manyika, J., 119, 139, 149
Marot, M., 160
Martin, J. A., 22, 115, 116
Masley, S., 67
May, T., 86
McCann, J. E., 11, 12, 19, 23, 25, 27, 29, 37, 49, 66, 88, 90, 97, 100, 104, 121, 126, 142, 150

McLean, B., 28
McNealy, S., 167
Menzies-Lyth, I., 62
Meyer, A. D., 28
Mihm, S., 85
Mintzberg, H., 114, 127
Mirabito, A. M., 64
Mitroff, I., 91, 145, 169
Moore, K., 85
Moran, E., 163, 164, 165
Murray, H., 21
Mytelka, L., 124

N

Nadler, D., 21, 26
Nagireddy, C., 62, 63
Nocera, J., 55
Nonaka, I., 88, 162
Normann, R., 49, 141, 159

O

Opie, R., 134
O'Shea, T., 10
Overdorf, M., 28

P

Pace, D. A., 191
Parise, S., 96, 150
Parker, B., 43, 160, 166
Pasmore, B., 10
Pearson, C. M., 169
Penenberg, A. L., 133, 135
Perrow, C., 28, 169, 171
Peters, T. J., 21, 57, 114, 127
Pichette, P., 119, 139
Pierce, C. S., 56
Pink, D., 56, 76
Porac, J., 87
Porras, J., 56, 57, 75
Porter, M., 22, 43, 74
Pritchard, J., 68e–69e, 70
Prusak, L., 23, 88
Putnam, H., 58
Putnam, R. D., 72

Q

Qualman, E., 163, 164
Quinn, R., 60

SUBJECT INDEX

Page references followed by *fig* indicate an illustrated figure; followed by *t* indicate a table; followed by *e* indicate an exhibit.

A

A&DC, 78

ABI Research, 165

Accenture, 103, 111

The Act of Creation (Koestler), 132

Adaptation: corporate approach to environmental, 5; "failure of collective action" for, 4; managing continuous change, 25*fig*–28; managing episodic change, 24–25*fig*; off-shoring and outsourcing strategies of, 26, 31–32; shifting meaning of, 5

Adaptive capacity: benefits of openness relative to investment in, 29*fig*; definition of, 19*t*; how High AR develops, 17–18; how race for agility stretches organization beyond, 37–38; making the case for agility and resiliency required for, 178. *See also* Change; High AR building

Adaptive design framework: Being Action-Oriented feature, 109, 113–115; Capabilities Design Cycle for, 117*fig*; description of, 22–23; designing around strategic capabilities for, 115–116; intro to Being Action-Oriented capability, 14*fig*, 15, 47–50; intro to Being Aware capability, 14*fig*–15, 43, 46–47; intro to Being Networked capability, 14*fig*, 15–16, 51–53; intro to Being Purposeful capability, 14*fig*, 42–43; intro to Being Resourceful capability, 14*fig*, 15, 50–51; Roll-up/ Rollout Capabilities Model for, 116–119, 118*fig*; Walmart case study on application of, 183–188. *See also specific capability*

Adaptive design mindset, 109, 113–115, 131, 181

Adrenocorticotropin (ACTH), 60

Afghanistan, war in, 5

"Agency problem," 74

Agility: agility in context of, 56; as AR (agility and resilience) element, 13; definition of, 19*t*; ecosystem level, 152; "The Era of Open Innovation" approach to, 26–28; how fragility is created during race of, 37–38; making

225